TIARAS AND TANTRUMS

Twenty-five years in service at Kedleston Hall

First published in Great Britain in 2010 by The Derby Books Publishing Company Limited, 3 The Parker Centre, Derby, DE21 4SZ.

ISBN 978-1-85983-770-2

Printed and bound in Cromwell Press Group, Trowbridge, Wiltshire

ROY ADAMS
TIARAS AND TANTRUMS

Twenty-five years in service at Kedleston Hall

CHAPTER
1

Kedleston Hall, four miles north-west of Derby, stands in 800 acres of landscaped gardens and parkland. An outstanding example of the neo-classical style, the Hall was designed and built in the third quarter of the 18th century as a great showpiece for the Curzon family. The north façade, 107 metres long, is arguably one of the grandest of its kind in Britain.

Whatever the brochure might say about Kedleston, the first view of the Hall comes as something of a surprise to most people. The house does not sit comfortably in its surroundings as Chatsworth does. The sun rarely shines upon the north front, which spreads coldly and austerely displaying a pedantic correctness of style. Dr Johnson, on his first visit, suggested the house 'would do excellently for a town hall'.

To a potential employee like myself, attending for interview in the early 1960s, the first glimpse of the building aroused only apprehension. Betty and I, in our hired car, had entered the grounds from the Village Lodge and started slowly up a winding drive through parkland dotted with ancient oak and beech trees. To our right the ground rose steeply to a fringe of trees on the horizon; to the left was a gradual descent to a brook which opened into a series of artificial lakes. A stone fishing lodge perched on the bank of the nearest lake. When the forbidding north front came suddenly into view, the scale and grandeur of the place was totally overpowering. I stopped the car with a feeling of dread in my stomach. Betty and I looked at one another in amazement. Had I actually applied for a job as houseman in a place this size?

There was no doubt that I had, for I carried in my pocket the original advert from the *Burton Evening Mail* and a letter inviting me to attend for interview. 'Houseman required for beautiful country home' the advert had stated. Immediately I imagined a charming and modest Georgian house with polished wood floors, a scattering of fine rugs and a longcase clock in the stairwell. I was not sure what being a houseman involved, but I assumed I would be a general handyman and was confident I could put my hand to most household tasks. I had over the years acquired other practical skills too, during my time as an apprentice painter and decorator before the war, and in the services during the war. I imagined that at Kedleston, after the day's work was done Betty and I would relax in the cottage which came with the job. I could see Betty wandering among gypsy roses in the garden while I sat with my sketchbook or perhaps attempted some wood carving.

Now, in an instant, the homely image vanished forever and a thought occurred to Betty and me almost simultaneously: this was not going to be a friendly place. But we continued on, still overawed by the spectacle before us, until the gradual ascent brought us close to the house. We turned left towards a group of outbuildings, passed under an arch connecting two brick-built mews blocks and entered a courtyard, where by chance and good luck we found ourselves outside the Estate Office.

I had barely turned off the ignition when a tall, grey-haired gentleman came hurrying out of the office. He walked round to my side of the car and tapped on the window.

'Mr and Mrs Adams?' He introduced himself as Walters, the agent, and continued 'I'm awfully sorry, but I'm afraid this job isn't for you. There's been some mistake.'

I looked at him in amazement. I was shocked and all I could do was to stammer 'What do you mean? I don't understand. Has the post been filled?'

'No, it's not that,' he replied. 'We've been looking for someone for eight months. The position's still vacant but you're really not the sort of people we want. I couldn't possibly offer it to you.'

He was bending down all this time and speaking to me through the open window of the car.

'But you invited us for interview just a few days ago. I have the letter here.'

'Yes, I know. And I apologise most sincerely for having brought you all this way. I'll pay your expenses, of course, but I'm afraid you're not the sort we're looking for.'

He made it quite clear, as politely as he could, that he did not want us and did not want to answer any questions. Then he tapped the car roof in a gesture of dismissal.

Being in a totally unfamiliar situation and still overawed by the surroundings, I did not know what to make of his remarks. Was he saying we weren't good enough for the job? Or, seeing us arrive in a motorcar, could it be that he thought us too good for the post? Perhaps he expected us, more in the manner of servants, to arrive on foot. Or was I possibly too old for the job? I was then in my 40s. Perhaps they wanted a younger couple. Then I began to feel annoyed. We had gone to the trouble of hiring a car, I had taken a day off work, we had come a considerable distance and here we were being dismissed before we had even got out of the car. I was determined not to be fobbed off so easily. I opened the car door, got out and spent a long time trying to persuade him to let us at least see round the house and tell us what the job entailed. At last he reluctantly agreed.

He led us along an outdoor passage, under the shadow of a small Norman church, and we entered the house by the servants' wing. We stood for a moment in a bare, flag-stoned hall from where a flight of steps led to the upper floors. We were then taken into a long, curving corridor with windows to our left and the facing wall covered with hunting trophies. Staring down at us were the heads of rhinoceros, antelope and a huge water buffalo, all of them dusty and uncared for.

Among them were cases of birds with moth-eaten plumage and faded labels stuck to the glass. On we went into another long, dark corridor with numerous doors opening off and which led eventually to a low-ceilinged hall with thick stone columns. The hall was dark and I thought we must be in some sort of crypt, until a glimpse through one of the few windows showed we were at ground level. A quick look round as we were hurried through revealed a series of classical busts in niches in the walls, then we were out into another corridor, and then another curving corridor. Here the walls were covered with armour. On the floor stood brass cannon and massive oak chests. On one chest I noticed a full-size Lewis machine gun.

At last our guide brought us to a kitchen where two people were at work. We were introduced to Mr Newton, the butler, and his wife, the cook. Mrs Newton was busy mixing ingredients in a large bowl. She gave us a cursory glance and went back to her cake-making, rather huffily I thought. Mr Newton was setting a tea tray. He stopped what he was doing and shook hands. Under the table three black Labradors slept soundly in boxes. At this point Walters suggested that Betty remain with Mrs Newton in the kitchen while the butler showed me round and explained the duties of a houseman.

Newton took me first to a room in the cellars where two boilers, each about 8ft long, provided a sort of central heating system for the family wing of the house. He told me my job would be to stoke and clean the boilers twice a day and on no account were they ever to be allowed to go out, even in summer. We then went back up two flights of stairs into the family quarters where he explained that I would have to clear the grates each morning in winter and set and light the fires, and make sure that the log baskets were full. This, more or less, was all the job entailed, apart from making myself generally useful when required and feeding a few hens. He told me that no one would bother me, that I would be left to myself and that I should keep out of his lordship's way at all times.

'Lord who?' I enquired, feeling I would get more information from Newton than I would from Walters.

'Scarsdale, the Viscount,' he replied. But the name meant nothing to me and neither did the family name, Curzon, nor at that time would any mention of Lord Curzon, had it been made. It was not something taught in history lessons at my school.

We returned to the kitchen and Betty and I were then taken to see the state rooms. Walters explained the house was open to the public on Sunday afternoons during summer and for occasional private coach parties during the week. He showed us round in a quick and perfunctory manner, rattling off the names of the rooms we went through: the Marble Hall, the Saloon, the Library, the State Drawing Room, the Music Room, the State Dining Room, and the State Bedchamber and Dressing Room. Up to this time my only knowledge of art had come from books, and the nearest I had been to fine paintings, sculpture, furniture and elegant living had been in the small number of Georgian houses I had helped decorate in Ireland. I would have liked to have spent much longer in each room but all the time we were uncomfortably aware that Walters did not want us there.

When the tour of the house was over he took us back to his office and I asked about the cottage. Again he was uncooperative, saying he did not want us to see it and he was sure we had seen enough already. Once again I insisted, and reluctantly he came with us to the village. We went in the car, Walters sitting beside me in the front seat. Leaving the parkland by the village gates, we drove down a narrow lane stretching away to the west. Walters directed us to a semi-detached Victorian building at the end of the village. As we approached we saw first that the garden was overgrown with waist-high weeds and then that the cottage was dilapidated. Perhaps dilapidated is not quite the right word. I had seen dilapidated cottages in Ireland, which despite their condition had charm and romanticism and every possibility of making something of them. I had nearly bought one. The Kedleston cottage, not to put too fine a point on it, was squalid.

Walters apologised for its condition, saying that it had been empty for eight months. Our impression was that it had been empty eight years. He fumbled in his pocket and produced a key but had no success in opening either the front or back door, so all we could do was to peer through filthy window panes at a grimy interior. Glancing up as we left I noticed a stone plaque set in the wall which bore a large letter S surmounted by a coronet with the date 1897 below.

Back we went to the Estate Office, where I raised the question of wages and conditions. Walters told us that the houseman would be required to work six days a week and go in on the seventh day as well to see to the boilers and light the fires. The hours were from 8 until 5 during the week, 8 to 12 on Saturday and two visits to the boilers on

Sundays. The wages were far lower than I was earning from the tanker driving I was doing at the time, delivering oil to farms in Staffordshire and Derbyshire, but included the rent-free cottage. Walters then said that if Betty helped out part-time in the kitchen the wages might perhaps be raised a few shillings.

We shook hands, thanked him, and told him we would think seriously about the position. His parting words were he did not expect to hear from us again.

During the next few days Betty and I gave the matter serious thought indeed. At the time we were living in a council house in Burton and both of us longed for the peace and quiet of the countryside. We had little money and no chance of buying a place of our own, so a job with accommodation included seemed the ideal solution.

Betty and I had met during the war. I was serving in the Royal Navy and she in the WRNS and our paths crossed in Belfast. I had proposed to her on my 22nd birthday in February 1944. We intended to marry in June that year, little realising that plans were afoot for one of the greatest invasions in world history. Our wedding had to be postponed for a week as the D-Day landings got under way and all armed forces remained on high alert.

Betty had been born in Northern Ireland to a Catholic father and a Protestant mother. After the war we lived for a number of years just outside Enniskillen. Our elder son Nicholas was born to the sound of battle drums. The date was 12 July, Orangeman's Day, 1946, and the drums were reputedly those used at the Battle of the Boyne. They were huge ancient drums which the drummers beat with short canes until their hands were bloodied. That was their privilege. Our younger son Richard was born just over a year later. When both boys were christened in Enniskillen Cathedral, the priest holding Nicholas in the vestry afterwards asked me for his date of birth. When I told him, he said: 'Had I known that, I would have christened him William, so I would.'

I worked as a painter and decorator for a time. But as an Englishman in Northern Ireland and hampered by the Catholic name of Adams, I found it difficult to survive let alone make any advancement, and after five years of struggling we decided to return to England.

I found a job in Burton working as an assistant at Curry's, a small family business at that time, selling bicycles, prams, radios and what was in the early 50s still a relative novelty: televisions. They had tiny 9in screens and the nearest thing to a colour set was buying a sort of plastic bag filled with coloured liquid which you fastened to the screen. I also carried out bicycle repairs in a shed behind the shop. I mended dozens of punctures everyday, repaired bells and lamps, replaced worn brake blocks and ball bearings, and fitted new chains. But then I fell ill with rheumatic fever and the firm found themselves unable to keep my job open for me.

During my months of convalescence I took to helping my father in his upholstery business. My Dad loved his work. I can see him now scooping up a handful of tacks, throwing them into his mouth, tap tapping away with his upholstery hammer and humming *Charmaine* to himself as he worked. He also made cushions, hoods and aprons for perambulators. You do not see many of those today, the elegant

Marmets with coach-painted bodywork and 18in wheels, or the Silver Cross with its C-sprung chassis.

Our first consideration now was the boys. Nicholas had by this time left school and was in the RAF and hardly ever at home. Richard was still at school. He lacked the adventurous spirit of his brother but was keen on the idea of moving to the country even though it would mean changing schools. The tanker driving I found tolerable enough. What troubled me was giving up banding. At the time I played the saxophone in Freddie Watts' dance band. We used to play at halls in Lichfield, Ashby, Burton and Derby. It was not a good band. The leading saxophonist was really a trumpet player and his technique was all wrong. During the war on home leaves I had played an alto sax but that had been stolen in sad circumstances. Freddie lent me a tenor saxophone while I saved up to buy my own instrument. As soon as I had enough cash I went to Birmingham and bought a Conn, the best make you could get. I had dreams of becoming a Charlie Parker. If I had not been a married man, I think I might have become a professional musician after the war.

Betty and I now discussed all aspects of the job: what we had seen, what it entailed and what we wanted at this stage of our lives. Betty, I knew, was dubious about the whole venture.

'We'll be cutting ourselves off,' she said. 'We've no car and there didn't seem to be any public transport. How do people manage to shop? We should have asked more questions.'

I knew she was right. But incredibly the upshot was we decided to go ahead and accept the post. What possessed us I do not know.

Everything so far had pointed against it: the inauspicious interview, the unfriendly atmosphere, a squalid cottage, lower wages, no banding, no day of the week entirely to myself – all for what amounted to, and would certainly prove to be, hard labour of the most menial kind. At the time perhaps it seemed the only way open to us to get away from the council estate. We had no particular desire to rub shoulders with the aristocracy. We needed the peace of the countryside not the rat race of the town. Our intention was to stay at Kedleston for perhaps two years and then, with luck, move on to better things.

CHAPTER
2

I began my first day at Kedleston Hall by walking the mile or so through the village and parkland up to the house. Betty had made me sandwiches and a flask of tea as I had no idea what arrangements, if any, were made for staff lunches. It was a bright September morning, chilly at that early hour and with more than a hint of autumn in the air. Above me Canada geese flew in perfect formation, returning from an overnight migration and touching down in their hundreds on the lake.

As I neared a fork in the road, where the drive from the main gates met the drive from the Village Lodge, I saw someone approaching on a bicycle and I decided to wait and make myself known. The cyclist turned out to be the man I had been instructed to meet – a Mr Tommy Brown, who was to be my guide and instructor for the next few days. Tommy was an estate worker employed outside in the park or on any of the other land or properties owned by the Scarsdales. It was he who had been called in to attend to the boilers and fires and to feed the hens until a houseman was appointed. As we approached the house together I sensed that I was being viewed with the usual attitude of a country dweller towards a newcomer: suspicion, in this instance mingled with some relief.

We went through the Hall into the family quarters in the East Wing and I followed Tommy down to the cellars, where our first task was to open the draught to the boilers. Next the sitting room fire had to be cleared and set. The equipment for this procedure was left ready the previous evening. It consisted of three large, clean dust sheets, one empty bucket, a brush and shovel for the removal of ash, two buckets of coal, one bucket of well dried sticks, a quantity of newspapers and three large baskets filled with dried logs. The family rooms, in common with all great houses, were on the first floor which meant struggling up two flights of back stairs with all this paraphernalia. Tommy, I noticed, suffered from a club-foot (childhood polio I presumed), and this part of the work was particularly difficult for him. We were not allowed into the sitting room without first covering the carpet with dust sheets, which we rolled out before us as we crossed to the fireplace, for all the world like lackeys spreading carpets before an eastern potentate. The fireplace contained a fine Adam grate of polished steel, two brassbound wooden buckets for coal and two open coffers for holding logs. These coffers, Tommy explained, had to be kept filled with logs piled as high as possible, and it was usual on most mornings to carry up four baskets of logs. With the grate being so large, care had to be taken to make sure the fire started well, so a full bucket of dry sticks was needed too. When the fire was lit we descended once more to the cellars to attend to the boilers.

The entrance to the cellars was through a concealed door on the ground floor close to the family staircase. This part of the cellars below the East Wing ran from the north to the south front of the house and consisted of a large entrance room and a corridor flanked on either side by three rooms fitted with wine bins and all with brick vaulted ceilings. The southern end of the corridor opened into another large room with a heavy oak door giving access via steps to the parkland. The two boilers were in a room to one side of the corridor at the south end. The room opposite had been adapted with a chute down which coke, coal and logs could be delivered. This fuel, Tommy told me, was delivered every Saturday morning by the estate men who removed the clinker and ash at the same time. The corridor and two rooms adjacent to the boiler house were lit with single electric light bulbs; the other rooms had no lighting. There was a tiny window in the entrance room and a similar one in the boiler room but both were blocked off so there was no ventilation in the entire cellar area. When I expressed some concern, Tommy told me it was not my place to question anything.

'You'll leave well alone if you've any sense,' he advised. 'Why should we care if them buggers don't?'

Because, I thought, it is our or rather my health which will suffer. But I did not want to argue with Tommy on the first day so I kept my views to myself. The whole atmosphere in the cellars was one of complete neglect and would have made exactly the right setting for a horror film with festoons of dust-laden cobwebs hanging from every ceiling and clinging to every wall.

The two boilers were covered in monkey muck, that is a coating of asbestos paste about 3in thick. With the draught being open the coke was now glowing red, and this we stirred with long splicing rods to loosen the hot clinkers. Arid and sulphurous fumes came from the burning coke which were choking us even before we began to remove the ash and clinker from the bottom. We shovelled this debris into a corner to await removal later. By now the fumes and dust were making my eyes water, and my chest felt uncomfortably tight and dry. When I asked Tommy why the tiny window was boarded up, he told me no draughts were to go upstairs into the family's living rooms. Next we gradually fed the fire with coke to raise the pressure needed to circulate hot water through the wing. The system had no motor pump to drive water up three storeys, each of considerable height, and the fires needed feeding every hour or so to maintain sufficient heat and pressure to drive the water round.

While the dust was settling we went across the corridor to the coke and coal room to chop sticks for drying on top of the boilers. After 10 minutes or so Tommy said that the dust had settled so we trundled half a dozen barrow-loads of coke across to the boiler room and filled the coal buckets ready for next morning. We also filled log baskets and barrowed more logs along ready for use. Each log had to be brushed free of dust and dirt before it went in the basket. Once again I asked Tommy about this procedure and was told not to concern myself with the whys and the wherefores. He said I would not be expected to do anything other than the most menial of tasks and certainly never be required to show any initiative. But I was appalled by the state of the cellars and decided that despite what Tommy was saying once he was out of my way I would introduce changes.

It was now about 10 o'clock and Tommy suddenly remembered the hens. One of the duties of the houseman was to let them out each morning, feed them and gather up the eggs twice a day. We collected a bucket of hot mash from Mrs Newton in the kitchen, and a basket for the eggs, and walked through the park to a group of outbuildings some distance from the house. As we went, Tommy, still very cautious, volunteered a little information about the Kedleston estate. It comprised, he told me, 13 farms and over 40 houses and cottages in Kedleston and the nearby village of Weston Underwood. He had worked here for nearly 30 years, longer than anyone else. He had two men under him and there were two gamekeepers, one of whom lived in a Georgian folly on Cumber Hill, the other at Ireton Lodge, the third and smallest entrance to the parkland. 'I've never known a houseman last more than a few months,' he added, looking at me with some pity.

The hens, I noticed, were housed in comparative luxury in a warm, dry, well-lit brick building which Tommy said had been used as a radio transmission base during the war. The building was large, leaving the hens, some 50 of them, plenty of room to scratch around, and it was equipped with well-made nesting boxes. There was no shortage of straw or grain, which was stored in a similar building nearby. This second building was decorated with fine landscape murals, painted, I supposed, by a soldier during the war.

We collected the eggs and took them back to the kitchen. Tommy told me that any surplus over and above what the cook required was sold to a local poulterer. Mrs Newton then gave us a cup of tea and some biscuits in the staff room. Tommy seemed nervous in her presence and explained that this perk was not to be taken as customary. It was granted only when it suited her and she was apt to be temperamental. I looked at Mrs Newton, her head buried in the *Daily Mirror*, and something in her demeanour told me Tommy was right. I thanked her for the tea, to which she replied with a shrug of her shoulders.

After our short break we made up the boiler fires once again, wheeled in fresh coke, split more logs for sticks and filled the log baskets. Tommy would now normally have left the house to return after lunch to make up the boilers. He would then go back to his estate work and return in the late afternoon to fuel the boilers for the night. This week he had been instructed to stay with me to make sure I understood the routine and had familiarised myself with the house and surroundings.

One other job Tommy had been asked to do, when the Hall was open to the public from Easter to October, was to keep the public toilets clean. This task was now to fall to the houseman. So, armed with a box of toilet rolls and a yard brush, Tommy took me along for instruction. The Gents' toilet stood between the house and the stables. It consisted of a walled-off area with two flush toilets and a urinal about 8ft long which was merely a wall painted with tar with a half drainpipe below and a 4in square drain in the corner – all open to the sky. There was an antique flushing system which had long since seized up. Grass was growing out of the cistern. Tommy told me these toilets were a relic of the army days, and it did occur to me as I reeled back from the overpowering stench that they had probably not been cleaned since those far distant days. All Tommy did now was to brush a few cigarette ends down the drain, and with toilet rolls not needed he suggested we got out of the place as quickly as possible.

We returned to the house where I was shown the Ladies' toilets. These were situated off the tea-rooms on the ground floor of the West Wing. The tea-rooms, originally the great kitchen of the house, were now used to serve light refreshments to visitors. On a huge stone above the fireplace had been painted the words WASTE NOT WANT NOT and roasting spits and an enormous cast iron kettle still stood on the hearth. Compared with the Gents', the Ladies' toilets were tidy but dingy. Later I was shocked to discover that some women were obviously none too fussy about what they left stuffed behind pipes or on the tops of the cisterns instead of in the receptacles provided.

At lunchtime Tommy and I ate our sandwiches in one of the potting sheds in the stable yard. Tommy, I decided, was a good chap, still somewhat reserved but, if I were any judge of character, an honest and reliable man offering well-intended advice. Through the open door of the potting shed I could see the tower of the small church, older by centuries than the house itself.

'What was here originally?' I asked Tommy. 'The church must have served some community years ago.'

'There was a village here once, clustered round the church. But they moved it brick by brick down to where it is now. Smithy, cottages, parson's house, a mill – the lot went. About 200 years ago by all accounts.'

My thoughts went out to those villagers and the devastating upheaval in their lives. I pictured them grumbling and cursing as wagon after wagonload of stone and timber came rumbling past and they could do nothing but stare in amazement at the classical columns, marble staircases and pediments which rose from the rubble of what they had known all their lives as the manor house. A Scotsman was much in evidence poring over plans on a trestle table. Dividers flashed in the sunlight as he added a wee quadrant here, a balustrade there. And Baron Scarsdale, or whoever was behind the grand scheme, was not slow to order the demolition of an eyesore which affronted his vision every morning from his bedroom window, every summer evening from his dining salon. The village, he declared, was as acceptable as a carbuncle on a bride's backside. Such habitations as were necessary would be rebuilt some distance away, out of sight, on low-lying marsh meadows beyond the acres of parkland, which even now Capability Brown was casting a professional eye over.

'Come on lad. No peace for the wicked.'

Tommy's words brought me back to the present. It was time to return to the boilers once more. Tommy then suggested a tour of the gardens and outbuildings.

We strolled through the formal gardens at the rear of the house. The south front, despite its central pavilion modelled on the Arch of Constantine in Rome complete with monumental Latin inscription, presented a far less forbidding aspect than the north. It was framed by mature trees which did much to soften the overall impression. It was only the main features of the garden which caught my eye on this first occasion: the orangery, an octagonal stone summer house, a sunken rose garden and the more modern amenity of a swimming pool which blended well with its surroundings, screened as it was by two rose-covered pergolas and sheltered on the north side by a covered brick walk which in earlier days had been an aviary.

'How many gardeners are there?' I asked Tommy.

'Only the one. Old Ted Sentence. You'll meet him soon enough.'

'But one man can't look after all this surely?'

'They won't put their hands in their pocket for more. Me and my men do the heavy work, the mowing and digging and hedge trimming. And Lady Scarsdale deadheads a few roses when the mood takes her.'

We were now approaching the mews area again. The yard was bordered on three sides by coach houses and the once magnificent stables with vaulted ceilings built to take 20 coach and riding horses, with space for four special hunters and living quarters for grooms and stable lads above. Through an archway was an adjacent cobbled area where the humbler workhorses had once been stabled.

'Does Lord Scarsdale ride?' I asked Tommy. 'Does he have a horse stabled here?'

'He used to ride to hounds but not any more. I doubt he could haul himself into the saddle now. A good thing too if you ask me. The last horse he had, Trojan, was a brute of a creature. It was all his fault, treating him vicious the way he did.'

We left the now empty stables and entered an adjoining yard surrounded by potting sheds, laundry rooms and washhouses. In what was once a joiner's shop Tommy pointed out a couple of broken-down bicycles, ladies' ones, which he said he was sure I would be allowed to use if I could knock them into shape. These, I thought, would be handy for me and Betty, when she started her work in the kitchens, in getting us to and from the Hall.

We were now, having made a circular tour, approaching the house once more. We passed a game lodge and climbed a few steps to the churchyard opposite where tombstones set flat in the grass were carved with familiar Derbyshire surnames: Yates, Eyre, Furniss – faithful retainers, I imagined, resting here beneath the cedars and yews of the churchyard.

Tommy pushed open the door of the church and we gradually acclimatised our eyes to the dark interior. The church was intended to serve the parish of Kedleston but Tommy indicated that the Scarsdales more or less treated it as their private chapel. I looked about me, by now bewildered with so much information and so many instructions to absorb. I decided there would be plenty of time to come back to the church later and examine the series of Curzon monuments dating back to the 13th century. What I could not fail to notice was the ostentatious side chapel which Lord Curzon had built to the memory of his wife. White Italian marble effigies of himself, dressed in his robes as Grand Master of the Star of India, and his first wife, Mary Leiter, lay recumbent side by side on a marble sarcophagus, the monument surrounded by an ornate ironwork grille.

At the end of the afternoon we collected more eggs and fuelled the boilers once again. Then Tommy and I said goodbye for the day. 'What do you think to it all?' he asked.

What did I think? I was exhausted mentally and physically and could scarcely frame a coherent reply. I walked the back to the village with weary steps and despondent heart, knowing that I would not be able to keep my feelings from Betty or bring her any good news. The size and extent of everything I had seen I still found overwhelming, but the strongest impression of all was one of pitiful neglect and decay, which I found difficult to comprehend in a house of this importance.

I knew at the end of that first day that we had made a terrible mistake in moving to Kedleston.

CHAPTER
3

The situation was no better the following morning. Betty and I had discussed the matter and lain awake far into the night, our thoughts confused, knowing we were wrong in choosing Kedleston as a refuge from the council estate. But the decision we had made was not easily undone. Richard had started at his new school and my job and our cottage were now inextricably linked. We felt we had no choice but to give our best for two years, say. Two years with the peerage would surely warrant references to better things?

At the end of the first week, Tommy went back to his estate work and I soon realised that I was to be left alone to do or not do more or less whatever I chose. If anything it was the wretched boilers who were my masters.

I quickly made a friend and ally of Newton, who was pleased to have a man about the house who was interested and keen to work. Anything

I asked for in the way of brushes, brooms and cleaning materials he willingly supplied, which was a blessing to me since the more I discovered about the house the more I despaired. Here I was in a fine Palladian mansion, shocked at what I was finding. Apart from the family wing and the state rooms, and even these left much to be desired, everything was run down and neglected. I soon established a routine for dealing with the boilers, the fires and the hens, told Newton where I could be found and set about my programme of improvement.

My main priority was to introduce some ventilation into the cellars by unblocking the two small windows. I started with the corridor window. The glass and framework had long since disappeared, leaving an opening stuffed with cardboard, rags and splintered wood. The whole mess was covered in cobwebs and a thick layer of dust. All this conglomeration I removed to expose a small underground chamber beyond, into which light filtered from an overhead grille. On the floor of the chamber was a carpet of rotting leaves and soil. I peered at it for a few moments wondering whether I should attempt to remove this layer of slimy, decomposing matter, when part of it began to move in an alarming way. For a few seconds I almost panicked. There was something inexplicable here. Then I realised that the chamber was home to a colony of ancient toads which I must have roused from their torpor. I squeezed through the tiny opening and dropped to the ground, where I sank ankle deep in the debris of leaves. Bucket by bucket I gathered up the creatures and deposited them in the gardens at the back of the house. Then, when the chamber was cleared, I made a wooden shutter which I could put up or remove as required.

The second window, in the boiler room itself, was more difficult to deal with. Apart from the heat and dust and ash in the place, ready-to-use coke was piled up beneath this window, beneath which I found a collection of old and damaged water pipes. This left little space for working. But after a few days I had air circulating and the room looking more ship-shape. With the two windows and the back door open, I was now able to set about removing the cobwebs and years of dust and dirt covering the whole area.

In the largest room in the cellars, set out on a trestle table some 20ft long, I discovered a contoured ground plan of a World War One battlefield. Examining it by candlelight (the electric wiring in this part of the cellar had rotted away), I made out British, German and French model soldiers of all ranks, with their mechanised units, set among ruined buildings, blasted trees and trenches complete with tiny sandbags and signs. This war game must have been very impressive when operative but now it lay abandoned, covered in years of dust. I decided to leave well alone. There were more important tasks requiring my attention.

The cleaning of the cellars was done piecemeal over a number of months. I was given no protective clothing of any sort, not even an apron, but I still had my BP overalls and I wore these for work. One room, below the family kitchen, had been fitted with a small stone sink and a hot and cold water supply, and it was here at the end of each day that I stripped and washed down as I certainly could not go home to Betty looking as if I had surfaced from a shift down the coal mines.

My other priority was cleaning the outside Gents' toilet. My concern here was for the amount of algae and moss on the floor which on wet days made the whole area extremely slippery. I could not understand why none of the visitors had complained. Perhaps they had, but nothing had been done about it, and I was not quite sure who was ultimately responsible for these toilets. If any visiting gentleman should fall and break his leg I did not want it to be my fault, with the possibility of losing my home and my job.

The heavy growth of algae on the walls I was able to scrape off and take away in buckets but the floors needed scrubbing with water, and as carrying a bucket at a time from the nearest water supply (either from the potting sheds or the tea rooms) was too slow and laborious I had to wait for heavy falls of rain to tackle this task. When the rain came I dug out my old Navy oilskins and went down on hands and knees, scraping away. I got some steps and climbed up to the cistern where what I had earlier thought was grass growing was now ripening into a crop of wheat. This I removed, replaced the valve, and managed to get the cistern working again. Then I scrubbed the drain and the walls with gallons of disinfectant.

Every Friday afternoon, in preparation for weekend guests, I mopped down the landing and main staircase in the family wing. The stairs were about 6ft wide and cantilever-built of Hopton Wood stone. When I first saw them I assumed their dark grey colour to be natural, until closer examination revealed them to be pleasant shades of cream and pink. I immediately set about with pails of hot water, soap and scrubbing brush, and I had them finished and made myself scarce just before Lady Scarsdale returned from a shopping trip. Newton told me later she had remarked: 'Good God! What has happened? I'm in the wrong house!' This I interpreted as a compliment.

As the weeks went by I slowly came to terms with my initial shock at the condition of many parts of the Hall and the estate in general. It became obvious to me that, without money and staff, houses such as Kedleston were bound to deteriorate. Sound management was also needed at the top. Lord Scarsdale had inherited as a nephew, not a son of the house, and he had no sons to help work the estate. Four expensive daughters demanded his time and attention and he had not, as I saw it, ever been particularly interested in running a landed estate. Social conditions had changed, too. The days of cheap labour and living off rents were slowly slipping away and in most cases had all but come to an end. Walters told me that in the early 1920s, towards the end of Lord Curzon's time, there were 32 people working in and around the house. Now there were only about a dozen, many of them elderly and some only part-time.

It was the Newtons who were the mainstay of such staff as there were. At the end of each day I had gradually fallen into the habit of popping into the kitchen to tell them I was about to leave and enquire whether there were any special instructions for the following day. After a few weeks this led to my sometimes being invited to stop and have a cup of tea with them. The kitchen was fairly quiet at this hour of the day. Mrs Gowan, who helped out with the more simple tasks, had gone home. Newton would have brought the tea tray down from upstairs and would be washing up at the sink. 'One of her ladyship's whims,' he explained. 'The butler and only the butler washes up every item they use.' Mrs Newton, unless there was a dinner party that evening, would not yet have begun the cooking. I would sit at the table watching them, and apart from enabling me to glean information about the Scarsdales, these visits gave me an opportunity to assess the Newtons and their attitude to the combined post of cook and butler.

They were both Londoners by birth, and from what I could gather had both been in service for most of their working lives. Mrs Newton I placed as middle-aged. She had a round, fresh-complexioned face and she wore her hair wreathed Germanic fashion round her head in plaits. I soon saw that she was a very good cook and that her life centred entirely around her work, but like most good cooks she was given to vast and rapid mood changes. These moods, combined with the aura of importance with which she surrounded herself, led me to conclude she was slightly mad. She rarely spoke, indicating her intentions, her disapproval or her annoyance with gestures often more eloquent than words.

She had three constant companions in the kitchen. These were Lady Scarsdale's gundogs, the trio of black Labradors: Tango, Thunder and Tarquin, who slept in boxes under the table. By rights they should have been with the gamekeepers, who might have trained them to be useful working dogs. In the house they were thoroughly spoilt. On high days and holidays Mrs Newton baked cakes for them – a sponge cake with lashings of jam and cream for Tango, a fruitcake for Thunder and a rich chocolate gateau for Tarquin, her favourite. The dogs were at times incredibly ferocious, especially Tango, the father of the other two. He was unnaturally fierce for a Labrador, I thought. Over the years he had gnawed a good 10in off the bottom of the kitchen door to get out and away to any bitch on heat or to savage the sheep which tenant farmers kept in the parkland. Mrs Newton was not a cat lover, and if ever the cat ventured into the kitchen she would set the dogs on it. One day the inevitable happened. I found the poor creature dying in the cellars. I could not bring myself to dispose of it in one of the boilers, where many of the sheep the dogs had savaged ended up, so I buried it in the gardens at the back of the house.

John Newton was about 10 years older than his wife. He was tall and of slim build. His sallow complexion matched well the sad and resigned expression that rarely left his face. In such free time as he had he was always anxious to be off to the plot of ground he had cleared near the hen house and where he cultivated asparagus, beans and strawberries for use in the kitchen. He told me that this activity helped keep him sane. At first I thought he was joking, but later at teatimes when the conversation came round to the Scarsdales he would surprise me by the bitterness of his feelings towards his employers. This seemed quite out of keeping with the image of the perfect butler which he projected at other times.

I could see that Newton was worn out and exhausted. Not only was he butler in the house with the numerous responsibilities that post involved, but he was also valet and footman and housekeeper. When he first took up his position, Lord and Lady Scarsdale had promised to get him a footman, he told me, or an under-butler but had made no serious effort to do so, and the more Newton felt himself imposed upon the more his resentment grew. What irked him most was that he felt his services wasted on privileged people who were contributing nothing to society.

While I was engaged in my battles at the Hall, Betty was having her own struggles at the cottage.

We had moved in a few days before I was due to start work. Back in Burton we had packed up all our belongings and were waiting for the people who had agreed to buy Betty's almost new gas cooker for five pounds and our Bechstein piano for one pound. There was no gas laid on at Kedleston and no room in the cottage for the piano. Eventually the van arrived, and all our furniture was loaded. Betty, Richard and I squeezed in beside the driver and we were off.

When we arrived we saw straightaway that no one had been sent down to repair or even clean the cottage and make it habitable. The van driver, as he unloaded, said nothing but I could tell from the way he looked at me exactly what he thought. His whole expression said: 'You bastard, bringing a woman to live in a place like this.' And I had to agree with him.

All I can say is that the place was disgusting. I realised immediately that had we been able to see over the cottage on that first day of the interview I would never have dreamed of taking the post.

A dank and putrid smell hit us as soon as we opened the door. Next we saw that the previous occupants must have lived in filth. Our first job was to sweep the floors and then scrub every surface that could be scrubbed. This revealed many faults in the floorboards and the poor condition of the doors and window frames. Whatever lino we came across we threw out, together with two army greatcoats and several filthy blankets stuffed round the hot water cylinder.

A fuse box was hanging off the wall half smashed, wires sticking out loose and unguarded. This fuse box also appeared to have burnt a hole in a door that touched against it. The staircase was in a poor state of repair and the walls up the stairs were particularly bad, which meant I had to renew large areas of plaster. Under the stairs was a small larder fitted with shelves; however, it was so damp that it could not possibly be used for storing food. I stripped it down to the brickwork and left it to dry out as best it might. Even more worrying were the problems in the kitchen. The cottage, being semi-detached, had a small fireplace on the dividing wall, sharing a chimney with its neighbour. At floor level to the right of the fireplace I discovered the brickwork was crumbling away, and when I removed the rubble I could see through into next-door's kitchen. I dealt with this with an immediate but temporary repair.

To the left of the chimney breast a stone sink had been fitted. This was in the darkest corner of the room and there were signs that the plumbing had been leaking badly for some time. It was also a health hazard, being crudely installed with no swan-neck trap for waste water. I removed the sink and taps and plumbed them in under the window. Another plumbing disaster was the drainage system from a recently installed bathroom. Whenever bath water was emptied, and we needed frequent baths, it backed up outside in the yard and one of us had to stand there and divert the water away from the kitchen door with a broom while the other endeavoured to control the flow from the bathroom. I reported this to the office, but as little interest was shown I dug up the yard and replaced the collapsed pipes myself.

'Aristocracy!' I fumed. 'Family going back to the Normans! And this is how they expect us to live.'

While I was dealing with major repairs, Betty was still cleaning, scrubbing and removing rubbish from inside and outside the cottage. In the garden we found two old milk churns, numerous buckets and pans, and a perambulator. For weeks we had huge bonfires burning in the evenings to dispose of more and more rubbish. Against the front walls of the cottage was a great mound of earth piled as high as the window sills. As I began shovelling this away a young boy came by. 'Don't touch that, mister,' he called. 'House'll fall down.'

Our furniture was far too big for the tiny rooms. We managed to squeeze the beds upstairs after removing the banisters, but the wardrobes and dining table had to be stacked in the hallway. I went into Derby one Saturday afternoon and bought new furniture, the smallest I could find, and even this when it arrived we could not get up the stairs without damaging it and the walls.

These early weeks were a trying time for us. Walters had promised to pay for any decorating materials but nothing came of his promise. The estate did contribute £10 towards the cost of a new fireplace in the living room; all other bills I had to pay myself. To ask for assistance in any form was useless. We should have complained about the state of the cottage but with everything to lose and no money behind us we were afraid to do so. Newton suggested I approach Lady Scarsdale. He felt sure that if she knew the conditions we were living in she would do all she could to put things right. But I had not even met the woman and it was certainly not my place to approach her directly. I had to follow correct procedure which was to go to Walters; and Walters blocked or ignored every request. We were learning to our cost the power held by master over servant in a tied cottage.

The village of Kedleston straggles along a half-mile stretch of lane leading away to the west. The cottages had been built on one side of the lane only with a screen of trees opposite them. The trees – limes, beeches and horse chestnuts – were planted by Lord Scarsdale's grandfather, who found the sight of staff cottages offensive whenever his coachman drove him from the grounds.

My cycle ride each morning – I had by now repaired the two ladies' bicycles for Betty and me to use – took me past, on my right, four pairs of cottages very similar to our own, then past the tiny Corner Cottage set down like a dolls house at the junction with Buckhazels Lane, then past another pair of semi-detached cottages and then, still on the right, past a larger and older detached cottage overgrown with ivy and for the most part concealed by yew trees. This cottage had a sinister aspect and the village children were afraid to go past it on their way to school. A witch lived there, they imagined, and the stories they invented about her made them even more frightened. Beyond this cottage lay what had once been the village cricket field with an old pavilion slowly rotting away. Whether the village could now muster 11 able bodied men for a cricket team was doubtful. Who provided the cricket ground for the village I did not know, but I assumed it was either Lord Curzon during the last few years of his life which he spent at Kedleston or Lord Scarsdale in the years before the war.

To my left as I cycled were fields where tenant farmers grazed their cattle, and beyond the fields was Cutler Brook running down from a trout farm about a mile upstream. I often caught sight of a heron waiting to dive upon fish that had escaped from the farm.

Next on my route at the sharp bend in the lane stood the finest house in the village, The Old Rectory, a brick-built Georgian mansion set in the marsh meadow adjoining the park. Opposite on the inner curve of the bend was Yew Tree Cottage. If now instead of turning in at the village gates I had continued on, I would have crossed a small bridge where Cutler Brook entered the parkland, and then come to Rose Cottage on my left opposite which stood a small Victorian school, provided, as a stone plaque indicated, by the generosity of the Honourable Sophie Curzon in 1867. Further still was The Smithy and last and certainly least a large and ugly Victorian house.

Lord Scarsdale had permitted his tenants to choose their own names for the cottages provided they kept to flowers or trees. Our cottage had no name and all the obvious ones – Rose, Honeysuckle, Jasmine, Primrose, Laburnum, Holly and Lilac – had already been used so we remained No. 12. Who lived in all these flowery cottages I had no idea. Betty and I had no time for socialising, and even had we the time and inclination we would have been hard pressed to establish contact with our neighbours.

Kedleston was quite unlike the idea of the traditional English village described by many of our writers or portrayed by watercolour artists of an earlier period. There were no thatched cottages grouped cosily together, no figures bent over garden gates gossiping, no village green and no church tower rising in the midst. Whatever community spirit may once have existed, I felt sure had disappeared at the end of World War Two. The chief fault, of course, was that the village had been removed from its focal point, the church, which was now situated a mile away on private land and cut off from the village by the physical barrier of the parkland fence. There was no shop, no pub, and the Victorian school, which might have served as a small village hall, had by this time been converted to a private dwelling. There was nothing, in short, to unite a disparate community.

I was more aware of who did not live in the village than who lived there. Tommy Brown lived at Weston Underwood two miles away, and old Ted Sentence, the gardener, lived at Quarndon three miles away. The Newtons occupied a mews flat up at the Hall. For the rest I knew only that Walters lived at Rose Cottage, opposite the schoolhouse. I assumed the curate of Kedleston lived at The Old Rectory; he never as far as I was aware made any attempt to visit his parishioners or extend pastoral care to them. The witch I had glimpsed once or twice and I saw that two elderly women, part-time cleaners at the Hall, lived at Village Lodge itself. Village Lodge, designed by Robert Adam, comprised two of the tiniest little houses you could imagine, one on either side of the gates. They consisted of a single room each so small I doubt you could have got a cow in as a byre.

This then was the village, or rather the hamlet, of Kedleston, only five miles from Derby in pleasant countryside but seemingly without a soul.

CHAPTER
4

I must have been in the house three or four weeks before I came face to face with Lady Scarsdale, but it was even longer before I met his lordship. Newton had instructed me to keep out of their way. They were not interested in me, he said. My function was to contribute to their comfort and the smooth running of the house while making sure I was neither seen nor heard. He did tell me, however, that in the event of my meeting unexpectedly with one or other of them and being spoken to, I should address them at all times as m'Lord or m'Lady.

I had spoken occasionally to lords and ladies before I came to Kedleston and I was not particularly in awe of my present employers. But I had noticed varying attitudes to them among the other staff. Mrs Newton regarded them as a god and goddess, to be worshipped with the choicest offerings her kitchen could provide. I could well imagine her sinking to her knees at their approach or salaaming low before them.

Newton, who came into closer contact with them than his wife, had a more realistic view as I had already observed. I had heard him curse them on more than one occasion. Walters, the agent, was terrified of them. He went in fear and trembling of doing or saying the wrong thing. He concealed the deterioration of many properties on the estate because he lacked the courage to tell them what was wrong and that money needed spending. It was Walters I held responsible for the state of the cottage we had to live in. Tommy Brown's attitude was one of necessary subservience in his chosen way of life. He had worked longer than anyone else on the estate and was the only one of the employees called by his Christian name.

I had by now got to know something of the daily routine of Lord and Lady Scarsdale without directly being part of it. This routine was: breakfast in bed at eight o'clock; luncheon in the dining room downstairs at one o'clock; and tea in the upstairs sitting room at half past four. In the mornings when I was about my work in the yard I would sometimes see Lord Scarsdale in moleskin trousers and an old tweed jacket, a gun under his arm, heading for the mews where his Land Rover was stabled. Lady Scarsdale would be in the house seeing to the flowers, answering her mail and generally keeping an eye on things. After lunch she exercised her dogs in the park. On Monday mornings she consulted with Mrs Newton about the week's menus. On Tuesdays and Fridays she drove into Derby to order provisions, Newton explained, and sometimes to visit the auction rooms.

One morning I was leaving the Trophy Corridor when Lady Scarsdale came round the blind corner and there we were, face to face.

She could have swept by and ignored me but she chose to stop and say a few words.

'Oh, you'll be the new houseman.'

'Yes, m'Lady.'

'How are you getting on?'

'Very well thank you. I'm beginning to find my way around.'

'What's your name?'

'Adams, m'Lady.'

'Well, keep up the good work Adams. If there's anything you want, ask Newton.'

And she went on her way.

My first impression was of a woman of striking good looks and one not entirely unsympathetic in manner. The short mundane conversation, scarcely worth recording in other circumstances, marked the beginning of my relationship with a woman I came to know extremely well over the years, to be in one sense on intimate terms with while always maintaining my position as a servant.

I was told Lady Ottilie Scarsdale was Austrian by birth. I imagine the family left Austria just before the war. When I first met her that day in the Trophy Corridor she must have been in her 50s. She was always to maintain great secrecy about her age, almost an obsessive secrecy. Many years later when I had occasion to look in her passport I discovered she had effaced the year of her birth even on that document. In her youth she had been a great beauty. Barbara Cartland at one time compiled an anthology under the title *Book of Beauty and Health*, which contained photographs and thumbnail sketches of the women she most admired together with comments on their lifestyles. Of Lady Scarsdale, by then in her 60s (or so we presumed), she wrote:

Tilla Scarsdale can sit on her long, thick, shining hair.
She also has the most perfectly proportioned figure and
moves with a grace which is sheer delight and very un-English.
She is so essentially feminine that her deep matter-of-fact
voice is a surprise.

Lady Scarsdale attributed her good looks to being breast-fed for eight months; taking plenty of exercise – two to four mile walks each day; drinking sparingly, a brandy and ginger ale twice a week; and going to bed early. Barbara Cartland also made brief mention of Lord Scarsdale as 'the most adventurous, handsome and exciting young man of the 20s and at one time the best pistol shot in the world'. The entry concluded with the comment: 'Kedleston Hall is the background for so many of my novels and Tilla is my idea of a breathtakingly exciting heroine'. Looking round me I found it hard to believe she was writing about the same place.

Richard Curzon, the second Viscount Scarsdale and 29th Lord of Kedleston, had succeeded to the title in 1925 on the death of Lord Curzon, his uncle. The ancestor they shared was the Revd Alfred Curzon, fourth Baron Scarsdale, Lord Curzon's father and Richard's grandfather. Grandfather's presence was still strongly felt about the house and in the village, both in tangible ways and even more by repute.

Richard Curzon was born in 1898. His early years followed a predictable course for a young aristocrat: Eton, Sandhurst and a commission in the Royal Scots Greys. His date of birth meant he saw some service in both World Wars – in France and Belgium and Germany in 1918–19 and in the Middle East in 1941–43. In the Library was a photo of him in Cairo in army uniform, obviously enjoying himself immensely. As Barbara Cartland said he was a very handsome man, though not particularly tall. After World War One I believe Lord Curzon secured him some employment but he stuck it for only a few months before taking to the role of young man about town, following the popular pursuits of the 20s: motor racing at Brooklands, polo at Hurlingham and big game hunting around the world. Both Tilla and Richard had been married before and had children by their first marriages. I assumed they met in London towards the end of the war. Richard had looks and a title; Tilla brought a dowry with her.

My first encounter with Lord Scarsdale took place in the cellars. It was gone five o'clock on an afternoon in early October. I had just changed out of my overalls and had washed and was ready to go home when his lordship entered.

'Oh, good. You're still here. I'm looking for a tin of rat poison. It's down here somewhere.'

We were in a part of the cellars which had not yet received the benefit of my cleaning programme. The walls were lined with bins but it was many years since they had held wine. Into them had been crammed all sorts of rubbish: broken crockery, old greasy saucepans, damaged lamps, bits of wood and much unidentifiable waste.

'What does it look like, m'Lord? I'm afraid I haven't got round to cleaning this place yet.'

'Oh, it's just a tin. Get in there and have a root round.'

I must have spent about three quarters of an hour rooting around among the rubbish and filth, wondering where the rats were that he wanted to deal with. Eventually I came across something the size of a tin of boot polish but completely rusty and corroded so there was no saying what it had held originally. I showed it to him.

'That's it,' he said at once. 'Get it open.'

'But it's falling to bits, m'Lord.'

I had answered him before I remembered that it was not my place to query anything, merely to get on with it. Of course, the tin broke as I opened it and out fell something the size of a penny, resembling cracked and dried up leather. Anyone who could have identified what it once was would have been a clever man indeed. Lord Scarsdale looked at it with disappointment and turned and walked out without another word.

My first impression was not favourable but this is being unfair to a man who was usually friendly and courteous to everyone. His attitude to his staff was that they were there to serve him and it would never have occurred to him that they had lives of their own, far less to enquire into those lives. He never interfered with the running of the house or questioned methods or looked into the organisation. All he required was that everything he needed be placed before him exactly when he wanted it.

As the days progressed more and more, facets of life at the Hall were revealed to me. A particular recurring feature was the visit of a certain Commodore Jackson Whayman. Any information I gathered at the time came, of course, from below stairs. There his name was mentioned with affection and respect.

I remember well our first meeting. On the day of his arrival, Lady Scarsdale sought me out and asked in her most charming manner if I would make myself available to carry up the Commodore's luggage as he would be arriving earlier than expected and Newton would be on his afternoon break. A normal greeting from her ladyship would be giving me the time of day with perhaps a 'well done' thrown in for good measure. But here was a charming, excited, high-spirited woman asking, not ordering, me to attend on a VIP. This was a Lady Scarsdale quite unknown to me.

The Commodore arrived in a smart Sunbeam Talbot sports car followed by a small van containing his luggage. He was, I judged, about 60 years of age, my height but rather better built than myself. There was a definite twinkle in his eye as I was introduced as 'another sailor like yourself', and our handshake began a true and lasting friendship. He looked me in the eye, nodded and simply said: 'We'll talk later.' Then he and Lady Scarsdale went upstairs to the sitting room.

I carried his luggage up to No. 4 bedroom on the guest floor at the top of the house and then returned to unload the van. I was still puzzled as to why Lady Scarsdale had chosen to introduce me, the lowest of her servants, to a guest. Was it merely because I was new? And what lay behind the fellow sailor comment?

The van was filled with strong, beautifully made wooden boxes each neatly labelled with letters and numbers in what appeared to be a code. I had been given the key to the old schoolroom on the ground floor. This room was always kept locked and shuttered as it held other of the Commodore's possessions. I trolleyed the boxes along and stacked them as neatly as I could.

Newton had already filled me in on what he knew of the Commodore. He worked for the Cunard line, he told me, as one of their senior officers, captaining cargo vessels sailing between Britain and South America via Portugal, Madeira and the West Indies. These ships carried a few passengers and it was on one such trip, on a voyage up the Amazon, that he and Lord and Lady Scarsdale, who were taking a winter cruise, had met up. Soon a friendship developed between the three. 'Though if you ask me,' Newton said, 'it was encouraged more by her ladyship than Lord Scarsdale. He bellyaches whenever the Commodore's here. Still, it keeps her in a good mood for a week or two which helps us all.'

This was true. During the Commodore's visit Lady Scarsdale was transformed. Whenever I caught a glimpse of her, there was a new lightness in her step and she had kind words to bestow on everyone. Mrs Newton was instructed to prepare the Commodore's favourite meals, Newton always acted as his valet and everything was to be arranged to make his time at Kedleston as comfortable and enjoyable as possible.

On that first visit I saw very little of the Commodore but we did have our promised chat. He sought me out one morning as I was bringing logs up to the sitting room and asked me how I had come to be at a house like Kedleston. Then the talk turned to the war years and he wanted to know where I had served. I let him take the lead in the conversation, feeling it too forward of me to start asking questions about his life at this first meeting. But in answer to his questions I told him about the DEMS (Defensively Equipped Merchant Ships) and how I was a Royal Navy gunner serving aboard merchant ships of various types.

The Commodore's visits lasted from a few days while his ship was being turned round to a few weeks if he were changing vessels. He was never one for being idle. He exercised the dogs, he went shopping and he would set about painting in true naval fashion. Very soon I found myself involved in the painting side of things.

'Come on, Adams,' he said. 'If you've been in the Navy you must know how to use a paintbrush.'

So I left the cellar cleaning programme for the time being and together we started on some much needed decorating, he with a roller and myself with a brush. Sometimes Lady Scarsdale put on an overall and gave a hand too for half an hour or so. The Commodore even took it upon himself to order scaffolding from Derby, and between us we built a tower on wheels so that we could reach the high ceiling of the Tapestry Corridor.

The first task the Commodore and I tackled was the painting of Caesars' Hall. The hall took is name from the busts of 10 Roman emperors displayed in niches round the walls, and it was the low, dark part of the house which Betty and I had passed through on our first visit. It was at ground level in the very centre of the house, the main entrance being behind the five arches of the north front. The only windows, also on the north front, admitted no direct light and its low vaulted ceiling, supported on rows of massive Norman-looking columns, gave it the atmosphere of a crypt. It was furnished with four

Georgian settees, four drop-leaf tables, an enormous Victorian wind-out table which when fully extended could seat at least 30, a number of serving tables, two Adam stands for candelabras, some small chests and two magnificent stone jardinières set at the far end by the entrance to the Indian Museum. But despite all this furniture the size of the hall made it appear almost empty. Scattered over the floor were a number of Lord Curzon's lion and tiger skins. They were all in poor condition with teeth hanging loose in gaping jaws.

One afternoon we had stopped for a while and the Commodore and I were sitting on the floor, our backs resting against one of the columns. The bust of Nero gazed down upon us.

'You know, Adams,' he said. 'I am one of the fortunate few who are paid to do a job they really enjoy, whose work is actually a paid holiday. The only thing I can't stand is the type of passenger I have to mix with.'

His remark surprised me, since surely Lord and Lady Scarsdale were among just those passengers he was talking about.

'I prefer,' he went on, spreading out his hands before him, 'to be with people who use these, not the type my position forces me to socialise with.'

At the end of the day, after our exertions, he would say: 'I think that deserves a nip.' And he would produce a bottle of excellent Jamaican rum, not something you could buy in the shops here, and pour us a tot each.

Working together in this way gave us time to talk and slowly build a developing friendship. So far, I reflected, the arrival of the Commodore was the one good thing that had happened to me at Kedleston.

CHAPTER
5

In addition to my routine work and the programme of improvements I had devised, I was called upon from time to time to assist with various seasonal activities that life in a stately home occasioned.

The first of these tasks was the 'putting to bed' of the state rooms once the Hall was closed to the public at the end of October. This gave me an opportunity to acquaint myself with some of the many treasures these rooms held. Carefully I began wrapping all the small pieces in tissue paper or newspaper: the porcelain decorating side tables and mantelpieces; the numerous pieces of silver, many of them Indian silver presented to Lord Curzon during his Viceroyalty; the inkstands on the huge desk in the Library; the framed photographs in every room; and the obelisks and vases worked in Blue John, a rare type of fluorite banded with blue and yellow, unique to Derbyshire. When this was done Tommy Brown was called in to give a hand with some of the heavier work, so once again we were thrown together. It was good to be working with Tommy as my days were lonely ones apart from time spent with the Commodore.

Together Tommy and I now moved the furniture in the state rooms in such a way that we could roll up the carpets wherever possible and so protect them from dust. The largest carpet was the one in the State Dining Room, made for Lord Curzon's pavilion at the Durbar. The story was that relays of workers had produced in 60 days what would normally have taken two years to make. This we rolled up as far as we could towards the fireplace. Others were very old silk carpets, so soft we could fold them as easily as folding sheets. These we placed on the large Linnell settees, and the settees and all the other furniture we covered with dustsheets. With Tommy's help I climbed a tall ladder and took down the heavy curtains at the windows and closed the shutters. The curtains we placed on the floor, carefully wrapped in tissue paper interspersed with mothballs, and then stored them in large chests, either those in the Armoury or in purpose-made curtain chests kept in the semi-state bedrooms on the top floor. When this was done I turned my attention to the steel grates, fenders and fire irons.

The established routine here was to smother the bright work with Vaseline and then wrap everything in newspaper. This procedure had been carried out haphazardly for a number of years, resulting in part bright, part rusty steel with crevices packed with black and hardened Vaseline. Even the pair of wonderful Adam grates and fenders in the Marble Hall were in this same sad state of neglect. I now spent many afternoons cleaning and polishing and black-leading. It was dirty, painstaking work but rewarding to me when finished. Thereafter a monthly rub with wax polish kept them shining and they no longer needed to be wrapped out of season.

I was now informed that in winter the state rooms, the grand staircase and the corridors were heated by oil stoves and that it was my duty as houseman to fill and attend to these stoves daily. Lord Curzon had installed an elaborate central heating system throughout the state rooms but this was now defunct. There were about 15 Aladdin oil stoves, and having worked for BP I was well aware of the enormous fire risk they presented. Their lamps, kept burning night and day, consumed some 15 gallons of paraffin in about 24 hours, leaving little margin for error when filling them in the morning. Some barely lasted the 24 hours, and should I be delayed for any reason in attending to them, the wicks would smoulder and char, filling the rooms with smoke. I was well aware too that the fumes from these heaters were slowly damaging the oil paintings on the walls, many of which were in desperate need of cleaning and restoration. I stood in the Music Room one morning gazing at a Bassano so blackened it looked as if it had been varnished with tar. The title in the cartouche told me it was *Moses Strikes the Rock*, but all I could make out were a few faint traces of blue and red paint.

Attending to the oil heaters meant I had to work extra time on Sundays, seeing to them as well as the boilers. The work was gradually expanding to fill a seven-day week. There was never any extra pay for the time I put in at the Hall beyond my specified hours. My only reward was the satisfaction, pride even, in the gradual transformation I was achieving in certain small areas. Sometimes I was called back in the evenings if there was a function and additional fires had to be lit. I was even called back to help carry luggage upstairs for late arriving guests. I now began for the first time to have niggling worries that I was leaving Betty and Richard too much on their own, particularly at weekends. Betty did not complain. She still had her hands full trying to make the cottage more comfortable, but the more I was at the Hall the less time I had to help her at home.

Shortly after the closing of the Hall the shooting season started. I was now called upon to pluck and dress game birds, mostly pheasant, and skin a few hares and rabbits. This I did in a room in the cellars. It was a messy, smelly job as the game was always rather high and often badly shot and then mauled by the dogs. I had never plucked game birds before, but by trial and error I soon discovered the best way of going about it. The shoot met twice a week throughout the season with about eight guns attending, presenting me with upwards of 40 pheasants to pluck each time. The first shoot of the season, the big one, took place close to the Gothic Temple, a Georgian folly where the head-gamekeeper lived. Lady Scarsdale did not shoot – she did not approve of it, neither did the Commodore – but she always went out with the guns and enjoyed her duties as hostess and the social side of these occasions. They took their lunch in Caesars' Hall – usually oxtail casserole or jugged hare, followed by a rich suet pudding which Mrs Newton had been boiling for hours in a cloth. Lady Scarsdale, I noticed, appeared to have a soft spot for the under-gamekeeper, who was always smartly turned out and whom she declared to be her idea of the perfect gamekeeper and his wife the epitome of a good under-gamekeeper's wife. What characteristics went to make an ideal under-gamekeeper's wife I assumed to be a secret known to the aristocracy alone.

Betty by now had started work in the kitchen, helping out when there were big dinner parties or the Newtons were away. From the first the situation was difficult. Betty herself had been a professional cook and two such women in the kitchen was perhaps asking for trouble. It did not take much to set either of them off, Mrs Newton always full of resentment at imagined invasions of her territory, and Betty angry at the way we had to live and the lack of help or consideration shown to us. When the two of them clashed it was usually better to keep out of the way.

The Newtons had four consecutive days off at the end of every four weeks when they used to go down to London. Betty then would be asked to cook breakfast and luncheon for the Scarsdales. In the evenings they would try and get themselves invited out to dinner, or failing that they would repair to a local restaurant. Despite these arrangements it was obvious they regarded the Newtons' absence as a considerable inconvenience which threw their routine into disarray. Very soon Betty and I were asked to go up to the Hall and sleep there for four nights while Lord and Lady Scarsdale went to the International Sportsman's Club in London to be cosseted. The idea was that we would keep an eye on things in general and look after the dogs in particular. Mrs Newton, on being told of the plan, immediately took umbrage and made no effort to hide her resentment. This was hurtful to us, as we had no desire to steal her glory and were not even keen to stay in the house as we needed all the time we could muster to work in the cottage and our wilderness of a garden. By now we were well aware of Mrs Newton's dark and unpleasant moods. Before she left for London she would always put away all the kettles, pots and pans, and, worse still, as we discovered on the first of these visits, she locked the food away and took her big bunch of keys with her. There was nothing for us to eat except a jar of pickled eggs. I had to cycle back to the cottage and fetch bread, bacon, potatoes, butter and milk. And, not wishing to antagonise Mrs Newton further, we took our own pots and pans with us and even our own bedding, though we had been given permission to make full use of the house and its amenities.

Looking after the dogs was no easy undertaking. One of the dangers was that Lord Scarsdale allowed certain tenant farmers, in return for a monthly rental, to graze sheep and cattle in the parkland where they roamed freely. And given half a chance Tango, Thunder and Tarquin would be out among the sheep creating havoc. Already on a number of occasions I had secretly burnt or buried part carcasses which the dogs brought back to the house or Tommy found in the parkland. On one disastrous occasion they had savaged about a dozen sheep in a pen and an irate farmer had come complaining to Lord Scarsdale, threatening in future to shoot any black dog found worrying his sheep. Complaints were useless. Lord Scarsdale reminded him that his sheep were worth only a few pounds each whereas the dogs were worth £200 each and advised him not to take the matter further.

Bearing these difficulties in mind, I decided the first morning to take the dogs for their exercise in the gardens rather than the parkland. There were after all 22 acres of garden for them to run in. Tarquin was as strong as a horse and all of them were strangers to the lead, though I doubted my ability to stay on my feet with three of them straining at the leash. To reach the garden I had to negotiate the long Armoury Corridor and open and close four doors. The 50-yard run down the Armoury Corridor at once threw them into a very excitable state so that when I eventually managed to open the outside door they were away and out of sight in a flash. The gardens were separated from the park and from farmland by a ha-ha. My fear was for what might happen if they jumped the ha-ha. But help was at hand in the form of the old gardener, Ted Sentence. He had checked their mad rush and had them foraging for hedgehogs under the bushes. When I explained my predicament he had some advice for me.

'Use a firm, strong voice with them,' he said, 'and always bring a big stick with you. If you beat the ground in front of them before letting them away that'll quieten them down. The buggers are thoroughly spoilt. That's why they're so difficult to control.'

Mrs Newton has a lot to answer for, I thought. But I followed Ted's advice and found that it worked.

One afternoon a few weeks later I found Newton in the kitchen smiling, most unusual for him, at a card he held in his hand.

'I've just found this in the waste paper bin upstairs,' he said with a grin. 'It's priceless.'

He handed me a Christmas card obviously intended for the Scarsdales. It showed a picture of the Hall with the Adam Bridge in the foreground and three black dogs in full chase through the parkland, blood dripping from their jaws. The leader was marked 'Tango'.

About a week before Christmas I was told to pair up the best pheasants, unplucked, as Christmas boxes for the bank manager, the curate, the doctor and selected tradesmen. I wondered whether Betty and I might be given a brace; although after plucking some 80 a week I had taken an aversion to the damned things and certainly did not want to eat one on Christmas Day. One afternoon Lord Scarsdale came down to the cellars, gun under one arm, his other arm raised aloft grasping the long legs of a bird he had shot.

'Here you are,' he said, smiling. 'A meal for you and Mrs Adams.' And he handed me a heron.

I thanked him but as soon as he had gone I threw it on the fire. I had no desire to find out what heron tasted like.

The nearer Christmas approached the more apparent it became that I would get very little time off. The Scarsdales had a lavish programme of entertainment planned with guests arriving every day. So most of my time was spent keeping the boilers, oil stoves and open fires going, and carrying luggage upstairs for the visitors. Betty was helping Mrs Newton in the kitchen under strained circumstances and we had only a few hours to spend with Richard and our other son Nicky, who was home on leave from the RAF.

On Boxing Day morning the Meynell Hunt met outside the north front of the Hall. Lord Scarsdale allowed the public access to the park for a small charge, and over the years this had become a popular Boxing Day attraction. My part, as houseman, was to lay and light two large fires in Caesars' Hall and keep them blazing away. The hall was damp and cold and needed large fires to produce any warmth, but when they were lit the overall effect was quite pleasing. Once the fires were going well I went home, washed, changed into the smartest clothes I had and returned to help Newton. His job was to serve the punch and I helped him carry two huge solid silver Regency tureens by the silversmith Paul Storr, together with their matching ladles, from the strong room to Caesars' Hall. A disadvantage was that Caesars' Hall was a good distance from the kitchen where on these occasions Lord Scarsdale, assisted by Mrs Newton, prepared the punch himself. Into the mixing bowl went the least expensive wines from the cellar. Lord Scarsdale never gave anything away! But as soon as his back was turned Newton laced the punch with a bottle or two of Scotch. Lady Scarsdale saw what was happening and did not disapprove; she was never one for stinting her guests. Between us Newton and I carried the enormous tureens full of hot punch down the Armoury Corridor and down another corridor to Caesars' Hall. Newton ladled the punch from the tureens into glasses and I took the glasses out on a silver tray and handed the mounted horsemen and women the traditional stirrup cup. It required some skill to pass among the riders with a tray of glasses. I kept a wary eye on the horses' hooves and on the feet in the stirrups and the hounds sniffing around my legs. The punch received compliments; Lord Scarsdale told anyone who asked that it was a secret recipe handed down from generations, and everyone was happy. His lordship never drank so he was unaware of the little deception practised upon him.

Later as we cleared away the tureens and the glasses and left the fires to die down, I glanced out of one of the windows. It was snowing heavily.

CHAPTER
6

It was a terrible winter. Betty and I huddled round the wireless at every opportunity listening to Home Service news bulletins. Roads were blocked, power lines down, villages cut off, and cattle and sheep starved to death as farmers were unable to reach them with fodder. It did little to comfort us to hear that this was the coldest winter since 1740.

At Kedleston, as elsewhere, the Hall and village were cut off for days. It was impossible for the postman, the milkman or any tradesmen to get through. Cutler Brook and the lakes froze and there was that strange silence that snow brings – with no traffic, no birdsong, no shoots and most outdoor tasks coming to a stop. A few nearby farmers had managed with tractors to clear a path from the Hall to the Main Gate and to the Village Gate and through the village itself as far as the last cottage. Beyond that point hedges, lanes and fields were indistinguishable under deep drifts of snow.

Cycling to work was out of the question. I set off every morning at seven o'clock in freezing temperatures, and armed with torch and shovel I plodded along in the darkness. One morning I saw the gleam of torchlight ahead of me and I realised it must be one of the cleaning ladies who lived at the Village Lodge. She was elderly and frail and not really fit to work, but she was still expected to struggle up the drive every morning. No one thought of coming down in the Land Rover to fetch her. As I caught up with her I saw she was limping along with sacks tied round her feet, so I took her by the arm gave her what support I could and together we stumbled on, the sky gradually lightening but still grey with snow clouds.

Once arrived, I had to see to the boilers, carry logs upstairs and light fires in the family rooms. There was a good supply of paraffin stored in a tank in the stable yard so I was able to keep the oil heaters going in the state rooms, though with temperatures falling well below freezing each night the heaters did no more than take the bitter chill off the rooms.

Fetching logs and paraffin was one thing, but now Newton told me it was my responsibility to make sure the drainage holes in the roofs were kept unblocked and he suggested I go out on the roof and do what I could to clear them. In the very centre of the house in front of the great dome of the Saloon was a complicated arrangement of flat, leaded roofs covered with narrow duckboards. At regular intervals in the lead were holes some 18in in diameter to allow rainwater to escape, though quite where this surplus water went I never discovered. 'Take a wooden spade,' Newton said, 'then you won't damage the lead.'

I climbed through the window of one of the semi-state bedrooms at the top of the house and lowered myself on to the roof. Lead, holes and duckboards were now all buried in snow so I had to grope around and try with the spade to locate the drainage holes and then scrape the snow from them. The front pediment, the dome and the hipped roofs on all sides afforded some protection so, although it was bitterly cold, there was no immediate danger. But the hipped roofs of the main pavilion, and of the east and west wings, had a different drainage system. Here the tiles sloped down to gutters but there was nothing so vulgar as drainpipes to mar the clean lines of the external walls. At regular intervals along the gutters were holes, fitted with moveable covers which could be opened to allow excessive water to escape down what must have been internal drainpipes. Immediately in front of the gutters was a low retaining stone parapet and in front of this a ledge some 18in wide with no protection whatsoever between it and the 50ft drop to the ground.

I climbed through a low louvred door and made my way on to this ledge. Such a manoeuvre was terrifyingly dangerous in good weather but now, with the roof covered in snow and a piercing east wind blowing, only a madman or someone bent on suicide would venture out here. The surrounding miles of unbroken white landscape disorientated me and a strong feeling of the madness of my situation, of the madness of this whole monstrous house and how I ever came to be here, swept over me. For a brief moment I had a strong desire to step over the edge and drop to the soft and inviting snow beneath. But the moment passed. I knew the snow would not break my fall. There was only an inch or two covering hard compacted snow beneath. Gradually I shuffled my way along the ledge, bending over the low wall and reaching down to the gutters in an attempt to find the covers. Once I had located the first cover and then the next I hoped it would give me some idea of the distance between each and so make my task easier. Easier? No one but a fool would call this easy. Well, I was a fool. A fool to be up here like this and an even bigger fool to have brought my family to the house in the first place.

The snow lasted until the early days of March, when temperatures rose and a slow thaw set in. Gradually a strange green landscape reappeared and conditions returned to relative normality. Meanwhile, Tommy Brown had been called in for the annual task of polishing the fine oak floors of the state rooms. This was a job he always spun out as long as possible. He enjoyed being in the house, with the relative warmth it afforded, rather than based at what was called the Woodyard, an unheated 18th-century hunting lodge in a wooded area of the park where the estate men hung out.

It was now, as the days became warmer, that Lord Scarsdale asked me to look after his collection of arms and armour for him, to clean the various pieces and make sure they were in good order. The collection had been put together over many years since he was a boy and the displays contained a comprehensive range of body armour and fighting weapons, from early crossbows to Tommy guns. The Armoury Corridor, where the larger part of the collection was housed, was the ground floor of the quadrant which joined the main part of the house to the family wing. It was not open to the public.

Before I started this work Lord Scarsdale gave me a guided tour explaining what the pieces were, their names, how old they were and how they were used. To the right of the entrance stood a full suit of body armour dating to about 1400, while to the left stood another suit of armour beautifully etched and chased with a design of birds and flowers. On stands close to these were his two large, one-and-a-half-handed swords, 'bastard swords' he called them, one in heavy plain steel, the other lighter, springy and with a razor-sharp wavy edge. He advised me to wrap this one in towelling whenever I took it down for cleaning and I was always nervous about handling it. Hanging high up along the stone walls were various spears, pikes and halberds. Lower down hung steel breastplates, an early rectangular shield, several round wooden shields with traces of hide still on them and a fine damascened Persian shield. Also decorating the walls were many types of edged weapons: Toledo steel daggers, Solingen-bladed swords, claymores, rapiers and smaller swords – even African skinning knives, eaten away with age but still razor sharp. The helmets he had set on chests which stood against the walls. These included Cromwellian lobster pot and tail ones, Spanish morions, cuirassiers' close helmets, a cabasset with its border of studs in the form of small brass flowers and an early helmet with an adjustable nose guard. I could not remember all the names at the time, but later by reading about arms and armour in books and sale catalogues I became familiar with the various terms. There were also a dozen French muskets, probably spoils from Waterloo. Lord Scarsdale pointed out the names of the owners beautifully engraved along the narrow bayonets. To round off the display in the Armoury Corridor were four sets of twin-barrel brass saluting cannons, while on two large coffers he had mounted German machine guns from World War One.

Now whenever I had an hour or so free I used to take down pieces from the Armoury, a few at a time, and clean them with fine wire wool and oil them if required. Once I had worked my way through them I would go back and repeat the treatment every few months. When all the iron and brass had been cleaned and oiled and the sun came shining in through the tall windows, the whole corridor presented a dazzling display to the eye.

One afternoon Lord Scarsdale came along while I was busy there and pointed to a breastplate and the rectangular steel shield which he told me to take down. I followed him outside into the parkland, bearing the armour in much the same way as a mediaeval squire must have done for his knight. Seeing him armed with his Lee Enfield rifle, I felt slightly anxious. But he produced wire and some nails and told me to fix the breastplate and the shield to the trunk of a beech tree. Having satisfied himself that the shields were secure, he strode 30 paces away from tree, turned and fired at them. After one or two alarming ricochets from the curved surface of the breastplate, the bullets made small indentations in each piece but did not pierce the metal. Even so, I felt relieved he had not asked me to wear them.

The gun room was adjacent to the Armoury Corridor. It was a room 40ft long with two doors and a large marble fireplace. Being close to the schoolroom it may perhaps have been the children's sitting room in earlier days. But any elegance the room might once have had was now lost by its conversion to part storeroom, part workplace. In the centre of the room stood a fine mahogany table, its polished top disfigured with scratches, knocks and gun oil. One window bay had been fitted up with a workbench and a vice. There were two chests of drawers which held tools and an early oak linen press where Lord Scarsdale hung his shooting clothes. The wall facing the windows was fitted with racks to hold fishing rods and gaffs. Lord Scarsdale was a keen fisherman, though I thought it ironic that his own five lakes were so fouled with reed that he had to fish at Major Knowles' lake at The Burrows three miles away.

The two alcoves to either side of the fireplace had been converted to cupboards. In the one to the left were half a dozen big game rifles. The other was home to Lord Scarsdale's pair of Purdeys (a 21st birthday present from his mother and father), a Thompson machine gun and two army rifles. Decorating the walls were a Fitzroy barometer and a case of hawking accoutrements containing early leather hoods, some of them for large birds, others tiny ones for birds as small as merlins, together with jesses with silver bells. Sometimes after a shoot Lord Scarsdale would leave his Purdeys lying about uncleaned. Since I washed and cleaned the guns' boots and wellies it seemed perfectly natural for me to strip and clean the Purdeys at the same time. He never made any comment about this so I continued to make it part of my routine on shoot days.

In the Tapestry Corridor, immediately above the Armoury, stood a German black-and-white half suit of armour and a suit of Sir John Curzon, who died c.1400. There was also on display at the foot of the great staircase a collection of early family firearms, mostly sporting guns, inlaid with silver and brass popinjays of the Curzon crest. I remember two early blunderbusses and a pair of pocket pistols reputed to have been carried by the first Baron Scarsdale on the Grand Tour. My lord told me he carried his knuckledusters when on tour.

Then, with the Hall about to open again, Tommy and I reversed our earlier programme of putting the house to bed. We rehung curtains, removed dustsheets, rolled back carpets, cleaned chandeliers and set out the various ornaments. I longed to know more about the treasures around me, particularly those in the State Dining Room. I could not resist running my fingers over a magnificent silver Pilgrim's Bottle, embossed with the Curzon coat of arms and fitted with silver chains. It was a splendid, if over ornate, piece of silver standing some 18in high – no pilgrim had ever carried a bottle like this. It had been presented, so the label said, by the children of Queen Victoria to Lord Curzon on his appointment as Viceroy of India. I wondered if Lord Curzon had ever cast such appreciative eyes over this piece as I was now doing, presented as he was with magnificent gifts wherever he travelled; gifts from every town and village he passed through in India. Its companion piece was a silver cup and cover about the same height, which I believe was presented to him by the Queen herself. But not everyone held the treasures in the same respect as I did. The cleaning women bashing about with their brooms were doing considerable damage, I noticed, to the fine gilded merman feet of the Linnell settee in the State Drawing Room.

The Hall opened to the public at Easter. A table was set up in the Marble Hall where tickets sold at the Main Gate (for house, gardens and parkland) were taken. Lady Scarsdale sometimes sat there, graciously welcoming visitors and working at her tapestry-style needlework. She made cushion covers, bell pulls and fire-screens, some of which she sold to the public who went away thrilled to have a cushion cover embroidered by a peeress of the realm herself. She also sold golf balls retrieved from the lakes. She and the Commodore would go down with fishing nets, pull on their wellies, wade in and poke around in the sludge to see how many they could dredge up. They never came back with less than two or three bucketfuls, to sell for RSPCA funds. And if ever professional golfer friends of Lord Scarsdale were staying at the Hall she would get them to sign a few of the balls, and for those trophies she got a very good price.

As time went on I became increasingly disillusioned with my role at the Hall. It was tedious and back-breaking work; although both Walters and Newton had suggested quiet hidey-holes to which I might slip away unnoticed and relax for a while when things became too much. But it was this very lack of accountability which worried me. As long as there was warmth and hot water provided, no one concerned themselves as to what I might be up to. There were numerous places to hide oneself away at Kedleston but I never followed up Walters' suggestion to malinger. Left to myself, I was more intrigued to explore areas of the house which no visitor would ever see and which few of the staff were even aware of. I soon realised that the design of the house was far more than a series of large interconnecting rooms arranged symmetrically round the Marble Hall. There were doors off corridors which led to secret staircases, doors off the rooms behind which were dark unseen chambers, there was a hidden walkabout high above and around the Marble Hall, and dreadful crevices down which a body might slip and never be recovered.

I even climbed to the very top of the house and into part of the roof itself. I had never seen so much timber in my life. Large though the roof area was, I could not stand upright anywhere but had to bend or climb over massive oak beams, 200 years old, bearing the tremendous weight of lead and tiles above, while smaller timbers of all sizes crossed and traversed each other in a seemingly random network, though, of course, there must have been mathematical principles behind the construction. It was quiet up in the roof apart from the occasional creak of timbers settling themselves as the temperature changed. But if I allowed my imagination to wander I seemed to hear voices, orders being shouted, curses exchanged, the grinding of pulleys as dozens of men hauled and manoeuvred the timbers into position and the tap, tap, tap of mallets driving home dowel pegs. Men must have been killed here, I had no doubt of that, either falling to their deaths or crushed when timbers slipped.

Friendship with the Commodore lightened the burden of my days at Kedleston, but as the two years which Betty and I had allotted ourselves drew to a close so our frustration mounted. We were both bitterly disappointed with the place and wanted to be away. We could have looked in the columns of *The Lady* for a combined residential post of cook/handyman but we had Richard to consider. He was now 17 and had left school and was working in the sports department of the Co-op in Derby. He also had a girlfriend he had met at a folk music club. We thought it unfair to uproot him from his job and separate him from the girl he was eventually to marry.

So for the time being it was press on as best we could and see what tomorrow might bring. Tomorrow, as it happened, brought something entirely unexpected.

CHAPTER 7

In the summer of 1964 the Commodore visited Kedleston during one of his long shore leaves. On this occasion he had taken on the task of painting the railings which surround the forecourt of the north front. It was a dirty, messy job, and rather than go into the house for morning coffee he had asked Newton to take a tray out to him.

One morning when Newton was otherwise occupied I was deputed to take coffee out to the Commodore. As I approached with the tray he greeted me with a smile and said: 'What's this, Adams? Have we got a new butler?'

'No sir,' I replied. 'Newton is busy and has asked me to do the honours.'

I rested the tray on a plank he had set up between two step-ladders and began pouring his coffee.

'I think you'd make a good butler, Adams,' he said as he wiped paint from his hands.

'Well it's not that difficult, is it sir? It's only opening doors, announcing "Dinner is served" and passing a few plates round.'

We both laughed. I knew this was not true. I was merely indulging in banter with the Commodore. But his next words took me entirely by surprise. Becoming serious, he asked me if I knew that Newton and his wife were leaving and that Lady Scarsdale was looking for a new butler. I was amazed. Although I was aware that Newton was getting on in years and working himself to the point of exhaustion, it had never occurred to me that he might retire. But the Commodore assured me it was true and told me the Scarsdales were finding it difficult to get a replacement couple. He went on to suggest that I could easily do the job and that it would be far preferable for me than the work I was doing then. He told me to think it over, leave it with him and he would see what he could do. I found the whole episode unreal. What had started as light-hearted banter had within minutes turned into a serious possibility.

With the cottage now more comfortable though still damp (the larder under the stairs never did dry out completely), Betty and I sat down once more for a serious discussion. It seemed obvious to us that if I were asked to become butler, Betty would be invited to be their cook, the new Mrs Newton as it were. The Scarsdales had never found fault with any of the meals she had prepared for them and would have been pleased to have her work full-time. But Betty was adamant that she had no intention of becoming cook. She still felt resentful that we had come to such a disgusting cottage where hardly anything had been done to help us. The cottage was part of my wages but I am sure we had spent far more on repairs than we ever would have in rent. Betty was always telling me that I was too soft and that she certainly was not going to put herself out for them. She would do no more than work part-time occasionally, but she had no objection to my becoming butler should it be offered and if it was what I wanted.

The following day Lady Scarsdale took me aside as I was returning from the hen house with a basket of eggs.

'I suppose you know, Adams, that the Newtons are leaving us.'

'The Commodore mentioned it yesterday, m'Lady. I was very surprised to hear the news.'

She went on to say how pleased she and Commodore Whayman and his lordship were with what I had contributed to the welfare of the house and that they felt sure I would make a good butler and they were now inviting me to take Newton's place. She continued with a list of inducements explaining that I would be given a large flat in the mews, I would receive a rise in wages, meals would be provided as would the correct dress for the position, that I would meet all sorts of interesting people, that I would, like Newton, get about £200 a year in tips, and when I left she would supply me with a reference which would take me into any house in the country.

I was not so big-headed as to imagine that it was on merit alone that I was being offered the post. I knew from what Newton said that it was extremely difficult to get a butler to work in any out-of-town house. City work was the thing that was wanted, and among the small number of genuine butlers still in the profession many had an aversion to working for the aristocracy. Wealthy businessmen were considered far better employers, and best of all was an appointment as a board-room butler. The Scarsdales must have already applied to Lines Employment Agency without success. I shall never know whether the idea of considering me had occurred to them or whether it was purely on the Commodore's recommendation that I was offered the post.

Despite my banter with the Commodore I knew that the position would be hard work with heavy responsibilities placed upon my shoulders. I had seen how Newton, although almost born and bred to a lifetime in service, had become worn out and exhausted by his duties. But my present post was hard and dirty work and involved long hours, and I was not afraid of hard work particularly if it should lead to a better way of life in the long term. I had some feelings of guilt that if I accepted the post it would be Tommy Brown, half crippled with polio, who would again be called upon to service the boilers, the fires and see to the hens until a new houseman was appointed. But, putting that aside for the moment, the main consideration in favour of my accepting the post was the prospect of £200 a year in tips. Simple arithmetic told me that if Betty and I could live on the basic wages, and there was no reason why we should not since we would have little free time to go out spending, then in five years, if guests were as generous as Lady Scarsdale had indicated, we would have a thousand pounds behind us, enough to buy a small house outright. That is what persuaded me to accept the offer. We now set ourselves a five-year term with the carrot of a house of our own dangling at the end of it.

The Newtons had given a month's notice and more than two weeks of this period had already passed. There was much to do.

First of all I required a morning suit of pin-stripe trousers, black jacket and waistcoat, and an evening tail-suit with white waistcoat, stiff shirt and white tie. I naturally thought that these would be provided new. But not so. Unknown to his lordship, Lady Scarsdale went through his wardrobes and turned out two old suits which appeared to date back to the 20s and were several sizes too large for me. Much to my surprise, she took me to a tailor in Derby to have them cut down to fit. I stood in the tailor's shop in acute embarrassment as he measured me and began marking out in chalk the alterations that needed to be made. Ten days later I returned, tried on the suits and found they fitted perfectly.

As far as I knew Lord Scarsdale never missed his suits; although some years later he asked me one evening as he was dressing to go out if I knew where his black pearl waistcoat studs were.

'I'm sorry, m'Lord, I don't recall ever having come across them but I'll have a look round and see if I can find them.'

I spent a long time searching his boxes and dressing table drawers until it suddenly dawned on me that I was wearing the pearl studs and had been everyday since I'd been given his waistcoat. I thought it best to say nothing. He never looked closely at what I was wearing and in a few days would more than likely have forgotten the incident.

It was Lady Scarsdale who informed the Newtons that I would be taking over as butler and she arranged for me to spend the last week of Newton's time at the Hall with him being shown everything that related to the job and instructed in procedure.

John Newton was perfectly happy with this arrangement but Mrs Newton made no effort to hide her disgust. I could understand her feelings. I imagine Newton had spent many years gradually working his way up from houseman to footman, to under-butler in various houses before eventually reaching the eminence of butler, whereas she saw me coming entirely without experience in this sort of work and securing the post of butler to a distinguished family in only two years. Her displeasure found an outlet in thwarting us of any attempts to look round their mews flat into which Betty and I would be moving when they left. Lady Scarsdale had suggested that Betty go round and measure the windows in case we should wish to put up new curtains, but Mrs Newton refused outright to let us in.

The days I spent as John Newton's shadow were exhausting. Everywhere that he went, I went. Everything he did, I watched and tried to remember. I made copious notes. He advised me to make a detailed inventory of all Lord Scarsdale's possessions, and to keep a diary of everything I did, and to note down precise details of any movement of chattels within the house, particularly of items kept in the strong room for which I would be the key holder. He pointed out that in the event of trouble, diaries and notes would not prove innocence but would point to diligence and concern for responsibility.

Following his advice, I kept diaries for nearly 20 years during my time at Kedleston – but the only one that survives is the one I feel least inclined to read again. In it, in addition to my duties at the Hall, I recorded the painful details of Betty's fatal illness and my own feelings at the time.

Newton instructed me in many basic rules. He told me the correct way to enter a room was to knock and go straight in. One did not wait for 'Come in'. This occasionally resulted in my seeing something untoward, but of course I attempted to retain my composure at all times. Similarly with any conversation I might hear at the dinner table. Lady Scarsdale herself had a few words to say on this subject.

'I must warn you, Adams,' she said, 'that anything you hear at the dinner table is to be regarded as strictly confidential. And please don't take offence at anything you might hear said of servants.'

I am not particularly phlegmatic in disposition, but I think I managed to retain my composure in most situations I found myself in over the years, whether comic, exasperating, disconcerting or downright infuriating.

One afternoon had to be given over to checking the contents of the strong room where items of gold, silver and jewellery not in everyday use were kept. Inside were three large display cabinets and numerous boxes and chests for the smaller items. Like most rooms not in regular use it was musty and full of cobwebs.

Walters came along with the inventory and began to call out the items listed. Newton searched the cases and chests to find them and when he did so I signed for them. We began with the diamonds. There was an 18th-century parure, or suite, of necklace, pendants and earrings. This had been given by the first Baron Scarsdale to his wife, Lady Caroline. When we moved on to the silver I began to feel out of my depth. At that time I did not know an etui from an epergne. All I could do was trust Newton and sign. The most splendid piece of silver, in a case of its own, was a massive centrepiece which had been made from the winnings of a racehorse called Jason in the 18th century. The base was a silver and mirrored stand. Above this was a filigree bowl from which a dozen branches spread out. There were numerous attachments in the form of sweetmeat baskets and dishes which could be hung from the branches and there were dozens of little butterflies and other insects, all in solid silver, which could be disposed about the piece. Above this stood Jason, the Greek hero not the horse, carrying the Golden Fleece.

It was a Friday evening after dinner when the Newtons finally worked out their notice. Mrs Newton left early without a goodbye. John and I checked and secured the family wing in the usual manner and then walked through to the back doors which he locked for the last time before handing the keys, and those for the strong room, over to me. He gave me some last-minute advice, we shook hands and said our goodbyes. As I cycled back to the cottage to help Betty with the packing I reflected how it is often only when saying goodbye that one realises how much one has undervalued a friendship. Whatever the failings of Mrs Newton, Newton himself had been good to me, helpful and considerate at all times.

I started my new duties the following morning. The Newtons were due to leave that day, but it was late in the afternoon before they finally departed and Betty and I had the first opportunity to look over our new home. We were aware that Mrs Newton used to spend most of her spare time in the staff room and only went over to the flat to sleep, but we were quite unprepared for what we found when we eventually entered the place.

It was filthy. We saw to our dismay that it had not been cleaned or dusted for years and was in an appalling state. After our experience at the cottage this was almost the final straw. I consoled Betty who was in tears and told her that if they wanted me to stay then this time they would have to help us.

I went immediately to Lady Scarsdale and informed her in no uncertain terms what my thoughts and feelings were. I think she was scared I was going to hand in my notice then and there. The Newtons' resignation had already been a shock to her. To lose a butler, as well as the inconvenience involved, meant loss of face among other well-to-do families in Derbyshire, some of whom were unable to keep a butler at all. So there was, from her point of view, an element of one-upmanship to sustain. For the first time since I had been at Kedleston I felt I had some bargaining power.

Lady Scarsdale said 'Leave it to me, Adams. I'll sort it out.'

She told me to carry on at the cottage for a while longer and promised to get the flat cleaned and decorated throughout for us.

The following morning, Sunday, at the first opportunity during a break in my duties I went quickly across to the flat. I wanted to see if it really was as bad as we had imagined. The flat was one of two in what was known as the mews on the first floor above the stables. It was a large flat, its main feature being an 80ft-long corridor from which the sitting room, bedrooms and bathroom led off. The kitchen was at the far end. The long mews block was divided by a central archway, through which coaches had once passed, and the flats were approached by a communal stone staircase built into one side of the archway.

I climbed the first part of the staircase and found my way barred by a pile of old and dirty carpet-runner. I clambered over this mess to find even more of it blocking my path on the landing, while other carpets were hanging over the banisters. Trying to keep clean (I was of course wearing my morning suit), I eventually reached the door of the flat and opened it. An enormous cloud of dust greeted me. At first I could see nothing at all through the dust but I did detect a movement somewhere within. As far as I knew Betty had not intended to come to the flat so I called out to see who was there, and after a while a ghost-like figure emerged through the dust. This dirty dishevelled figure I eventually perceived to be none other than Lady Scarsdale herself, wearing what appeared to be an expensive tweed suit. Her long hair, usually so well coiffured and arranged elaborately on top of her head, was all over the place and her suit appeared to be ruined.

As soon as she saw me she called out: 'Don't come in here, Adams. You'll get filthy.'

'Well, come out yourself then,' I replied. 'Just look at the state of you.'

All niceties of address went by the board in my concern for the woman. It was not a fit place for anyone to be in. With little experience of cleaning, Lady Scarsdale had gone at it with a vengeance and stirred up all the more dust when it needed damping down. But I had to admire her for pulling the long runner out of the flat and throwing most of it downstairs.

She was as good as her word. She had two estate men remove all the other carpets and clean the flat. Then she called in an outside decorator to paint it, had the place recarpeted, and when all was ready she sent a vehicle and trailer down to the village to bring our furniture and other belongings up to the Hall.

Now at last, I thought, we might after two years of miserable conditions live a little more comfortably.

CHAPTER
8

Our new flat was certainly more comfortable than the cottage. But there were disadvantages. Along the length of the 80ft corridor were tall leaded windows, the original 18th-century windows still with original glass. These were by now somewhat ill-fitting which made the flat cold and draughty in winter. Their fragile condition was due both to age and to the fact that during World War Two a cluster of bombs had fallen at the end of the stable block. The German pilots were some miles off target, for presumably their mission was to bomb the Rolls-Royce factory in Derby where Merlin engines for Spitfires were manufactured.

But for the time being there were more important things to worry about than a draughty flat. I had a new routine to master.

My days now began at 7.30am and the first task each morning was to open all the ground floor shutters in the family wing. Next there was breakfast to serve. Lord and Lady Scarsdale always had breakfast in bed in their respective rooms, except when there was more than one visitor staying. On these occasions Lord Scarsdale would come down to the dining room to breakfast with his guests. If there was only one person staying, house rules dictated that breakfast was taken in bed.

My routine with the trays seldom varied, but I remember well the first time I served breakfast. At three minutes to eight I collected Lady Scarsdale's tray from the kitchen, climbed the flight of marble stairs to the first floor, and at eight o'clock precisely I gave a light tap on her bedroom door and walked in. The room was in total darkness since it was both curtained and shuttered. Still holding the tray I went smartly across to the windows. Like Newton before me I soon learned to cross a darkened room without stumbling into anything. I put the tray down on the table between the windows addressing Lady Scarsdale at the same time with: 'Good morning, m'Lady.' I then drew the curtains and opened the shutters. By this time Lady Scarsdale was sitting up in bed and I placed the tray on her lap. Her breakfast never varied: a pinch of cornflakes, a glass of orange juice and a pot of tea. I usually made some comment about the weather in the way of small talk and then proceeded through to her dressing room and bathroom, opening the shutters as I went. On the first morning she said to me: 'Well, here we are, Adams. A new beginning for both of us.'

I was at first disconcerted to notice that she slept naked. She might occasionally pull a bed-jacket round her shoulders when I went in but more often than not she did not bother. Sometimes the telephone on her bedside table would ring while I was still in the room and her answer to whoever it might be at the other end was always an indignant: 'I can't speak to you now. I'm naked.'

Lord Scarsdale liked a cooked breakfast: bacon and egg, or devilled pheasant, or kidneys, or perhaps fish, followed by toast and marmalade and tea. He was always called at 8.15. On the first morning when I went in with his tray he said to me:

'Look here, Adams, I'm the head of this household and if there's anything you want to know come and ask me. Always come to me first. If you've got any problems tell me about them. Look on me as a father. You tell me your troubles and I'll tell you mine.'

This seemed to me a strange way to talk to one's butler, though I must admit that I had no experience of how butlers were spoken to. I never felt inclined to tell him my troubles but over the years I did ask him questions about the house and his family history, and he was always pleased to talk if I chose the right moment.

After giving Lord Scarsdale his tray I gathered up the clothes he had worn the previous evening and put them to one side to be taken down to the pressing room. I then enquired what clothes he would be wearing that morning and laid these out ready for him. In my early days newspapers and magazines were delivered to the Village Lodge and brought up to the Hall by one of the 'dailies'. I was required to take the papers to the bedrooms as soon as they arrived. Lady Scarsdale would be up by this time but his lordship, unless he was going to London or out shooting, would be finishing his breakfast. It was at these times, if he was in the right mood, that we would have our little *tête-à-têtes*. We covered many subjects from news headlines to Curzon family history. I would have liked to have asked him where the money came from for the building of the house originally. I wondered whether it might be from slave trading.

He loved to reminisce and sometimes he told me about his first wife, who lived in London and whom he visited occasionally, and his four daughters. He also told me of his lifelong passion for boxing, and how when he was too old to box himself he had become a leading referee, and later played a considerable part in the administrative part of the sport, eventually becoming Vice-President of the British Boxing Board of Control. He would laugh when he remembered speaking against Lady Summerskill's private member's bill in the House of Lords to ban boxing. 'Stupid woman, Adams,' he would say. 'I told her quite plainly I'd been knocked out many times in the ring and the effects lasted only a few hours. I've also been thrown from my horse many times and suffered for weeks. So on those grounds she'd have us ban hunting too, I suppose.' At other times he would tell me how in his younger days if a poacher was caught on the estate he gave the fellow two options: being reported to the police or going a few rounds in the gloves with him. 'They usually chose the gloves,' he would say, 'and got the thrashing they deserved.'

Early on I became aware that Lady Scarsdale did not like us talking together, and if ever she came upon us engaged in conversation she always broke up our little chats by saying to him: 'Now, darling, don't keep Adams talking. He has work to do.' At which point I would take my cue and depart.

At some time between 9.00 and 9.30 the post arrived. As it was a considerable distance from the butler's pantry to the bedrooms (it was a three-minute journey along two corridors, up a flight of stairs and across a landing) I endeavoured to save leg-work by having his lordship's clothes brushed and pressed and his boots and shoes cleaned and polished ready to take up with the mail. This was not always possible as often his moleskin trousers would be caked with mud and needed a lot of time spent on them. I must say that his boots, when I had finished with them, would have passed any sergeant major's inspection.

After I had taken the post up to the bedrooms I brought the breakfast trays down to the pantry. There was a strict rule in the house that anything handled by the butler was washed by him. This meant that since I handled every piece of china, silver and glassware involved in the serving of food and drink and its consumption, I also washed all those pieces and was responsible for any breakages. This, I think, was a rule invented by Lady Scarsdale for the protection of her fine antique porcelain which was used everyday. I cannot imagine a butler in a more orthodox household spending as much time as I did washing up.

It was usually about 10 o'clock before I had my own breakfast. In the first few weeks I had sometimes tried to have a cooked breakfast a little earlier than this but more often than not I would be called away to attend on Lord or Lady Scarsdale just as the meal was ready. This was aggravating to me and a cause of annoyance to the cook who had prepared my breakfast. So we decided I would make my own arrangements and have breakfast in the butler's pantry at a time when

I was least likely to be summoned. Every day I had two Weetabix with a spoonful of glucose sprinkled over them, and a cup of tea. My break lasted 10 to 20 minutes depending on how much there was to do and I looked at the previous day's *Daily Telegraph*; although the only part I read was the Arts section.

After breakfast I cleaned the silver. First I cleaned the flatware: knives, forks, spoons and serving utensils. These were all Georgian silver. The knife blades were steel and had worn as sharp and thin as razors over the years. These blades stained every time they were used and had to be cleaned with special powder. After the flatware came the vegetable dishes from the night before, the table ornaments and a silver tea service.

I cleaned the silver in the butler's pantry where I had two large tables pushed together on which I could spread out the equipment needed. There was a blanket, folded in several layers, which was quite black, impregnated with silver dust from constant rubbing. If I were pressed for time, a quick rub of each item on the blanket would suffice. When I had more time I made my own polish from jewellers' rouge, ammonia and methylated spirits. The ammonia was to remove stains and the meths was a drying agent to ensure that the ammonia did not stay on the silver too long. I applied the polish and rubbed it in with my fingers. Newton had taught me to do this. He told me that before the war men were employed in some London houses to do nothing but clean silver. They used their bare fingers and wore gloves when they were not polishing silver so that their hands did not become rough. On repoussé work I removed the residue of polish from the crevices and hollows with a soft brush. Then all the silver was rinsed under running water and wiped dry with a soft cloth. The Kedleston silver was in immaculate condition. It had been well cared for over the years and had acquired a wonderful patina. I was determined to maintain it in this condition.

The Scarsdales rarely took morning coffee, although if guests were staying I might be required to serve coffee and then clear and wash the cups. About midday I would take a bucket of ice up to the sitting room, clean the small bar there and check that it was adequately supplied with drinks. Then I would set the dining table for lunch.

A large, round sequoia table of tremendous weight stood in the centre of the dining room. I might be tempted to say that at meal times this table groaned under the weight of silver, except I cannot imagine that anything would cause the massive sequoia piece to groan. Even for a modest two-course lunch for the two of them the table was resplendent. The centrepiece was a solid silver equestrian statue of George V. Around this I set four 18th-century candlesticks (though with no candles in them at lunch time). Then I put out a pair of silver gilt pheasants, about a foot long, and beside each place-setting a small box. Lord Scarsdale had a Charles I snuff box with fine engraving and Lady Scarsdale, in addition to her box, had a Charles I wine taster which she used as a receptacle for pips or as an ashtray. There were two heavy Georgian silver salts (from a set of eight), two muffineers for pepper, two mustards and a sugar caster each. I then set out wine glasses, water glasses and the cutlery. The dining room was on the ground floor adjacent to the kitchen and the food came through a hatchway. I never stayed in the dining room while they were eating; it was not the done thing.

After lunch when they went upstairs to the sitting room I would clear the table. The cook would scrape the leftovers from the serving dishes and perhaps put some aside for me. I then washed the plates, cutlery and glassware and put them away. Next I would ask the cook what the evening meal was to be and go back and set the table for dinner. I would change the covers, change the glasses, put out fresh napkins and this time put candles in the sticks.

At some time, either late morning or after lunch, I would set the tea tray. This was not a butler's tray as such but a large papier-mâché tray fitted with folding legs so that it could be stacked away when not in use. When I had finished all these tasks, usually some time after two o'clock, I was free until 4.15pm. Mostly I spent my off-duty time teaching myself more about art and antiques, particularly silver. I am afraid I had no energy or inclination to maintain the small garden Newton had cultivated and this soon became overgrown.

I went back at 4.15 and put the finishing touches to the tray. The cook would have prepared sandwiches, cut bread and butter, and set out scones and slices of home-made Battenberg. I loaded the tray with silver teapot, milk jug and sucrier; then two cups, saucers and plates, and silver cutlery; next came larger plates with the sandwiches and cakes; in winter there was a muffin dish with a container for hot water beneath to keep the muffins warm; and lastly the item which caused me most concern – a hot water jug. This was a magnificent piece of silver by the American silversmith Pierre Harache but not a practical design for a jug. It was a tall, narrow vessel which tended to wobble and might easily topple over. At exactly 4.27 I would mount the stairs of the family wing with my heavily laden and precariously balanced tray, conscious that the main hazard was still to come. Lady Scarsdale's Staffordshire bull terrier was a dog of vicious and unpredictable temperament. If, as I entered the sitting room, Benny took it into his head to go for me then no one could restrain him from sinking his teeth into the black trousers of my morning suit. Lady Scarsdale had a length of heavy duty electric cable, half an inch in diameter and some 18in long, which she kept under one of the cushions on the settee. She would beat Benny with this whenever he had a go at someone. He could take it. His body was as hard as a rock but the beating only seemed to make him more vicious. The strange thing was that when Lady Scarsdale was not there he was as gentle as anything and would roll over to have his tummy scratched. At other times I suppose he regarded it as his duty to protect his mistress.

Tea was Lord Scarsdale's favourite meal. Lady Scarsdale always said it was because he had been an Eton schoolboy, and she talked of tuck boxes and muffins toasted by a study fire and a fag to wait on him as the highlight of a boy's day. Now, 50 years on, the teatime routine was just as important to him.

While the Scarsdales were having tea I went to his lordship's bedroom and set out his evening clothes. Then I fetched the tea tray, washed up and took more ice to the bar in the sitting room. His lordship used to make cocktails for Lady Scarsdale in the evenings. I would then check once more with the cook about the menu and put any wine that needed to be chilled into the fridge. In winter I would close all the shutters at this time. When everything was prepared for dinner and there was nothing else to be done I would go back to the flat, usually about 6 o'clock, have an hour to myself and then change into my tail-suit and return at 7.15.

The Scarsdales took dinner at 7.30 when they were alone and at eight o'clock when they were entertaining guests. At the bottom of the stairs in the family wing was a table on which stood a pair of lamps, and between them a silver ink-stand and the Visitors' Book. Beside this in a frame was a neatly written card which set out the times of meals: breakfast eight o'clock, lunch one o'clock, tea 4.30, dinner eight o'clock. Below this was written: WE WAIT FOR NO ONE. That was there for every visitor to see; they could not fail to notice it. WE WAIT FOR NO ONE. And this was followed to the letter.

Opposite the hall table stood a large gong. I had to strike the gong every lunchtime and every dinnertime even when only the two of them were there and they knew perfectly well what time it was. Newton had shown me how to strike the gong. You started very quietly, worked up in a crescendo and then faded it down to pianissimo. When there were guests staying after I had sounded the gong I went up to the sitting room, walked in, caught Lady Scarsdale's eye and announced in time-honoured fashion: 'Dinner is served, m'Lady.' I would then go down and light the candles on the dining table and take my place by the hatch.

I remember remarking to Betty how unnecessary I thought it was to have to dress in tails, stiff shirt and bow tie just to serve two people a two-course meal in their own home. Leonard Mosley entitled his biography of Lord Curzon *The End of an Epoch*. Having read this book I always considered that from the servants' point of view the Lord and Lady Scarsdale I worked for were the 'end' and the next Lord Scarsdale the 'full stop'.

After dinner I washed the dishes, turned down the beds, put out his lordship's pyjamas and took his day clothes down to the pressing room. Every night before I left I checked the silver. I had a note of exactly what I had taken from the strong room for everyday use. I could easily keep tabs on the larger pieces but I liked to account for all the cutlery as well. This meant I had to know exactly what pieces were on the breakfast trays, what was on the serving table in the dining room, what was in the pantry ready for use and what might have been taken up to the bedrooms. I never went back to the flat until every piece had been accounted for, and sometimes I was there until very late for the sake of one teaspoon which had gone astray during the day.

When Lord and Lady Scarsdale were on their own I would get away between half past nine and 10 o'clock. When there were dinner parties it was usually nearer midnight when I finished, leaving them to their cards and the locking up of the front door of the wing. If there were guests staying it might be even later when I left since there would be extra breakfast trays to prepare or the table to set in the dining room. Whenever male guests were staying I had to act as valet to them and brush and press their clothes in addition to Lord Scarsdale's.

These then were my new duties, although very few days were spent exactly as described above. Special functions, shooting parties, holidays, staff problems — all brought changes or disruptions to the routine. There were mishaps too, such as any household suffers. There might be a power cut ('Adams, get on to the Electricity Board and tell them if the lights aren't on in half an hour we will sue') or frozen or burst pipes. All these were difficult to deal with because of the size of the Hall and the value of the furnishings and paintings.

My task, as I saw it, was to keep the place running as smoothly and efficiently as possible and to make sure Lord and Lady Scarsdale suffered no disruption to their routine. When things were going smoothly they were charming and pleasant and I was treated almost as one of the family. But when things went wrong I was definitely an outsider.

CHAPTER 9

There is no doubt that my duties at the Hall would have been made considerably easier had Betty been willing to become cook. But she was determined to restrict her participation to occasional work in the kitchen and helping out in emergencies. So during my time at Kedleston I worked with a succession of cooks who seemed to come and go all too frequently. One or two left within 24 hours of arrival, some stayed a few weeks, some months, but always there was an uneasy feeling that any one of them might up and go at a moment's notice. Lady Scarsdale's instructions to me were invariably: 'For God's sake, Adams, keep the cook happy.'

Most cooks, I soon learnt, were temperamental by nature and at the same time strong characters. Butler and cook had to work as a team if possible, try and get on well together and make allowances for each other's shortcomings. As butler I certainly could not allow myself to be bullied by the cook. At the same time I was not in a position to issue orders directly to her. The cook was master in her domain of kitchen and storeroom. All I could do was pass on orders which came from Lady Scarsdale or make suggestions in a tactful way.

I must admit that Kedleston Hall was not the most inviting of places in which to work, and first impressions, as Betty and I had experienced, could be off-putting. For anyone without a car the place was cut off from the outside world, and none of the cooks who worked at Kedleston had a car. It was about a mile walk to either the Main Gate or the Village Lodge, and the country bus which passed the Main Gate was an infrequent service. So bicycle, taxi or a lift from someone with a car were the only practical means of getting out of the place.

I cannot say either that the kitchen would appear attractive to a potential employee. It was a large room, about 40ft by 20ft, with few mod cons. The floor was made of thick pine boards which I imagine had been laid down when the house was built in the mid-18th century. There were two electric cookers dating back to pre-war days and in front of these cookers, the spot which took most wear and tear, the floor boards were in a poor state. In my days as houseman, when I was in and out of the cellars below the kitchen, I could hear the boards creaking above and look up and see through the gaps. In the centre of the kitchen stood a long Victorian pine table, covered at some later date with green formica which was now shabby, even dirty, in appearance. The sinks were steel with old wooden draining boards and there were no tiled surfaces anywhere for easy cleaning. The walls were painted but had not been redecorated for many years.

Lady Scarsdale's procedure for hiring a cook was to phone Lines Employment Agency and perhaps when she was in London she might interview any candidate they put forward as suitable. The disadvantage of this system was that none of the cooks had seen Kedleston before they took up their appointments and I imagine Lady Scarsdale must have made the place seem far more attractive then it was.

I had been working only two or three days as butler when Lady Scarsdale told me she was planning a dinner party for the coming weekend. A function of this type had not taken place during my time as Newton's shadow so I felt I was really being plunged in at the deep end. In addition to this, we had no cook. No one had yet been appointed to replace Mrs Newton. Undaunted, Lady Scarsdale told me she would order a meal from a restaurant in Derby. It would be delivered hot and ready to serve. She would carve from the side table and all I would have to do was take the plates round.

'Remember always to serve from the left-hand side of each guest, and serve the guest of honour, the lady sitting to the right of Lord Scarsdale, first; then his lordship and then proceed clockwise round the table. There'll only be six of us so I'm sure you'll be able to manage.'

I was still apprehensive but then I took to thinking that if Lady Scarsdale was confident of my abilities, then it was up to me to be confident too. I believe she wanted to show me off, proud that she once again had a butler to serve her guests.

The meal when it was delivered was roast duck; three roast ducks, with accompanying vegetables, and profiteroles for pudding. I kept the main course hot in the oven and when they were all seated at table set the ducks upon a large platter and the vegetables in silver tureens and brought them to the serving table. Lady Scarsdale carved the duck and set out portions on each plate. As Lady Scarsdale carved, it became apparent that the restaurant had left packets of giblets stuffed into each bird (a corny old joke but not so funny now). Fortunately, the guests were too busy conversing to notice what was going on at the serving table. I carried the plates to each guest and went round with the vegetable dishes from which they served themselves. Then I retired to the kitchen, to return and clear away the plates when Lady Scarsdale rang. Next I served the profiteroles. Cheese and biscuits were ready in the kitchen to round off the meal and I made coffee and set it on a tray in front of Lady Scarsdale for her to pour. It was not so difficult after all.

It was another week or two before a new cook arrived. I took to Mrs Mumford immediately. She was an elderly silver-haired woman, gentle by nature and full of understanding. Earlier in her career she had been a lecturer in Domestic Science and Hygiene at a London college, she told me. The first thing she did was to banish Tango, Thunder and Tarquin from the kitchen and move their boxes out into the corridor. If she had any reservations about other shortcomings they did not worry her unduly since it was understood she had come only on a temporary basis and would be leaving in six weeks. Mrs Mumford was an excellent cook and we got on well together. Outside work her main interest was in church architecture and she was knowledgeable about cathedrals and the building of them. She showed me her collection of books on the subject and explained that she was on her way north to York and Durham to carry out further research. We became friends for the short time she was at the Hall and I was sorry to see her go at the end of her six weeks.

Following Mrs Mumford's departure we were without a cook for some time. Then came a couple who stayed only one night. The intention had been that he would be taken on as footman to assist me, and she was to be the cook. They arrived after lunch one day, looked round, inspected the kitchen, saw the rooms they were to occupy and said they were not staying. They seemed to me to be a couple well used to service. They gave no explanations. They merely told Lady Scarsdale they could not take the post and intended to leave early next morning. So my hopes of having an assistant were short-lived.

Next in sequence was a Scot, Miss MacDonald. Whenever a new cook arrived Lady Scarsdale always arranged for a taxi to bring her from Derby station up to the house. One Monday morning shortly before lunch I happened to be with Lady Scarsdale in her bedroom when we saw a taxi coming up the drive from the Main Gate.

'This will be the new cook,' Lady Scarsdale said. 'You go downstairs and welcome her, Adams, and then bring her up to me in the sitting room.'

We watched the taxi deposit a tall, slim, middle-aged woman and her suitcases on the forecourt of the north front and then turn and drive away. I made my way downstairs but by the time I reached the ground floor I found that Mrs Gowan, the kitchen-hand, had beaten me to it.

To be greeted by Mrs Gowan was a misfortune in itself. One look at her would tell anyone that she was below average in intelligence, that she was grossly overweight and she was none too clean. Gossip below stairs had it that her mother used to come to the village twice a week and take all her laundry away and bring her tins of food since she was incapable of washing or cooking anything herself. Even if she had put a clean apron on she would still have appeared slovenly, but Mrs Gowan never bothered about cleanliness. I recalled one occasion when she had been summoned for jury service. As soon as Lady Scarsdale heard of it she was on the phone to the courtrooms. 'You can't use her. She's a half-wit. She wouldn't understand what was happening.' As a result Mrs Gowan was released from jury duty but what, I wondered, was the poor woman doing in the employ of a peer of the realm?

She stood there now, crumbs round her mouth and rubbing her hands down her greasy apron before introducing herself to the new cook. I stood for a moment watching these two contrasting examples of womanhood – the slim, upright, prim and proper Scotswoman and the fat, slovenly, local woman – and wondered how on earth they would communicate let alone work together. I waited a bit longer expecting the new cook to come inside. I thought I'd give her a few minutes to look round the kitchen, and then go and introduce myself.

But by now Lady Scarsdale had become impatient. I heard her step on the stairs and saw her go outside to Miss MacDonald. I could hear them talking but not too clearly at first. After a while I realised voices were being raised and recriminations and remonstrations were leading to a full-scale row. Something had obviously gone very wrong.

Eventually Lady Scarsdale came back inside, upset and flustered.

'She won't come in, Adams. She refuses to come through the door. Go and see what you can do. She's talking about going back today. Good heavens, we can't have that. Take her over to your flat and give her a glass of sherry. See if you can pacify her.'

This was not the moment to say I did not keep sherry in my flat for distraught cooks or anyone else. When I emerged Miss MacDonald took one look at me, realised I wasn't Lord Scarsdale, and decided that perhaps she could talk to me and find a sympathetic ear. She had seen Mrs Gowan, she told me, and she had seen over her shoulder into the kitchen beyond and been horrified.

'What sort of a place is this?' she asked. 'I certainly wouldn't have come here if I'd known what it was like. That woman told me a pack of lies. Getting me to come all this way and then to find I'm back in the Dark Ages. And surely she doesn't expect me to work with that woman. I'll not set foot in the place.'

'Well you can't stand out here all day. The taxi's gone. Come across with me to my flat, have a cup of coffee, and then we'll see about making arrangements to get you back.'

I picked up a couple of her suitcases and we began to walk towards the flat. I thought it best to humour her and gain time. I pointed out that it was an old stately home and some allowances had to be made.

'I don't care about old stately homes,' she said. 'Cooking for two, they told me. I thought I was coming to a bonny wee house. That kitchen's no place for any cook to work. I expect decent standards wherever I go.'

When we entered the flat the first thing she spotted was the telephone on a small table in the hall. She immediately rang the agency and launched forth on another tirade, demanding to know what they were doing sending her to a place like Kedleston. Next she wanted to phone for a taxi to take her to the station.

'I'm getting the first train back. I'll not be treated like this. I'll not be taken advantage of.'

I tried to pacify her, to talk to her not as a butler but as a friend.

'Please, don't be too hasty. Let's give this a bit of thought. If you go now, where will you stay? Have you anything arranged in London? At least stop one night, make an early start in the morning, and be in London in good time to fix up some digs.'

She saw the sense of this and calmed down a bit. Eventually she agreed to go over to the house and have a look at the bedsit that had been prepared for her. By now I think she realised that she would have to stay the night. When she was settled in, Lady Scarsdale went down to talk to her again, trying to persuade her to stop on at least until she had found another job. Lady Scarsdale promised to do whatever she could to make things better in the kitchen while pointing out that it was an old house and they could not make all the changes they wanted to because of planning regulations. Lady Scarsdale was good at this sort of talk and at last Miss MacDonald, although she locked herself in her room, agreed to stay on a temporary basis.

The following day she ventured into the kitchen. The first thing she did was to give Mrs Gowan a look that would have shrivelled any normal person. Then she started her tour of inspection and everything which met her eye seemed a personal insult to her. She picked up a saucepan and brandished it at poor Mrs Gowan.

'What's this? What do you call this? Call it a saucepan, do you? I call it a disgrace. I want this saucepan cleaned. I want all the saucepans cleaned – and outside, not here in the kitchen.'

Mrs Gowan went off, ran the saucepan under the tap, which was the limit of her cleaning, and returned.

'What's this? Do you call this clean? I want that pan scrubbed with salt and vinegar until I can see my face in it. And when was this floor last cleaned? I want the floor scrubbed and all the drawers turned out and cleaned. And we'll have you in a spotless white apron tomorrow, and your head covered when you work in this kitchen.'

During the next few days I had many a quiet chuckle to myself as I watched this double act at work. But Mad Mac, as I called her, was right. The kitchen *was* dirty and far from hygienic, and I was pleased that someone else was trying to achieve in the kitchen what I had struggled to attain throughout the Hall during my time as houseman. When she eventually got round to preparing a meal I could tell at once that she was a marvellous cook. Everything was of *haute cuisine* standard, amounts exactly right, and the dishes beautifully presented. But while she was there it was always touch and go whether she would deign to cook a meal at all. She never regarded herself as employed by Lady Scarsdale but rather that she was doing her a favour by staying on at all. She had a fondness for locking herself in her room just when she was needed – and woe betide anyone rash enough to knock on the door.

Mad Mac was with us only a short time until the agency found her another job. Unfortunately, Christmas happened to fall within that short period. Normally the house would be full of guests with parties and lavish entertainments planned and, of course, extra cooking required. Lady Scarsdale, realising the precariousness of the situation, had cancelled all the invitations she had issued. Only the Commodore was celebrating Christmas with them.

Christmas Day was the busiest day of the year for me and I was lucky if I had an hour free to spend with Betty. On this occasion, although not quite so rushed off my feet as usual, I had been too busy during the morning to notice what was happening in the kitchen. When I went there at about 12.30 I knew immediately something was wrong. Lunch, or rather Christmas dinner, was to be served at the usual time of one o'clock but there was no cook in the kitchen, no ovens on, no enticing aroma of festive fare. I walked over to the stoves and saw a few vegetables had been prepared and were sitting there in saucepans of cold water. There was no sign of the turkey. I assumed Mad Mac must have started to prepare something and then taken it into her head that she was not going to do any more and locked herself in her room again.

Not daring to knock on her door, I paced up and down outside the room. I coughed. I banged about a bit in the butler's pantry which was adjacent to her room hoping to alert her to the time. After 20 minutes or so I ventured a timid knock on the door but there was no reply. For a moment it crossed my mind that she might have committed suicide but I quickly dismissed this as a melodramatic thought.

At 10 past one the Commodore came down to the kitchen.

'You haven't sounded the gong, Adams. Have you forgotten the time?'

'No, sir. I haven't struck the gong because there's no meal ready. The cook's not about.'

'What do you mean there's no meal? Where's the cook? What's the matter with her?'

'She's locked herself in her room and won't come out.'

'Well, sound the gong. Perhaps that'll rouse her.'

The Commodore went back upstairs to report to Lord and Lady Scarsdale. I struck the gong well aware that it would achieve absolutely nothing. After 10 minutes or so the Commodore came downstairs again.

'His lordship is getting very annoyed, Adams. And Lady Scarsdale has had nothing to eat since her few cornflakes at breakfast.'

I was getting annoyed too because the longer this went on the later I would be getting away to spend time with Betty, the less Christmas celebration of my own I would have. The Commodore now knocked sharply on Mad Mac's door.

'Miss MacDonald, please unlock this door at once. We are all waiting for you. Are you not well?'

Still there was no reply.

'Come on, Adams,' the Commodore went on. 'Let's get these vegetables on the go and see what there is in the fridge.'

'There's always plenty of eggs,' I said. 'And there's bacon too.'

I took down a large frying pan, scarcely believing that I was cooking bacon and eggs for Christmas dinner for the peerage. The smell of frying in the kitchen soon brought Mad Mac running from her room. She made no excuses or apologies. She merely said that the Scots did not celebrate Christmas. Hogmanay was their festival.

'Then if it's not a holiday for you, perhaps you'd be good enough to attend to your duties.'

It was the first time I had heard a note of sarcasm in the Commodore's voice.

After such a late lunch there was no Christmas tea, which put Lord Scarsdale in a bad mood for the rest of the day. Miss MacDonald prepared dinner that evening but it had been a long and trying time for everyone. She must have known exactly what she was doing. She was getting back at Lady Scarsdale in a spiteful way for having brought her to Kedleston on false pretences.

At about 10 o'clock I was in the dining room putting the last of the cutlery away when the Commodore came in.

'There's some whisky here, Adams,' he said. 'Pour yourself a drink before you go. You deserve it.'

I poured drinks for us both and he invited me to sit down with him.

'Merry Christmas,' he said, smiling at me.

'Merry Christmas, sir.'

Whether it was tiredness or the whisky I do not know, but for a few minutes sitting there in companionable silence with the Commodore I felt happier than I had for years. A friend was showing me kindness of a sort I had not experienced since coming to Kedleston.

CHAPTER
10

A few months after my promotion to butler, Lady Scarsdale received some sad news in her morning post. 'Oh, Adams,' she said. 'Poor Newton has died.'

She wrote a letter of condolence to Mrs Newton that same day. She was always prompt with her correspondence.

I was not surprised at the news. Already I was beginning to realise how great a strain Newton must have been under during his years at the Hall. With no footman to assist him, the butler was on his feet almost all day long, from early morning until late at night, running along corridors and up and down stone staircases. Once I became familiar with the various tasks – taking up the breakfast trays, cleaning the silver, washing up, setting the dining table, cleaning and ironing clothes – all these could be performed without much mental effort. The strain lay in anticipating what *might* go wrong and in knowing the course of action to put things right. Disruption was not easily tolerated by Lord and Lady Scarsdale. Everything had to be done correctly and punctually whatever the circumstances.

I now decided to do as Newton had advised and make an inventory of all Lord Scarsdale's personal possessions. When he was away in London and my duties were a little lighter, I bought a special notebook for the purpose and began to go through everything in his bedroom.

The bedroom was heavily furnished with antique pieces from Georgian to Edwardian times. A four-poster curtained with tapestries dominated the room. This had once been a fine bed but Benny, Lady Scarsdale's Staffordshire bull terrier, had the habit of cocking his leg up one of its mahogany posts, and the post and surrounding carpet were slowly rotting away while a stain crept up the tapestry valence. Lord Scarsdale regarded his furniture as he did his staff. It was there to fulfil its function, not to be considered or concerned about in any way. There was also a revolving Edwardian bookstand which held a collection of titles by Henry Miller which must have been risqué in the 1930s and 40s.

I now made a note of all his clothes: his suits, his outdoor wear, his underwear, his boots and shoes, and his hunting gear (though he ceased to ride long before I came to Kedleston), noting the condition of each item and where each was kept. The robes and coronet of his Viscountcy were locked in a large chest in the Tapestry Corridor, together with various bits of military uniform. After I had listed the larger items, I went through all the drawers and compartments of his gentleman's dressing table noting down combs and brushes, razors, cufflinks, tie-pins, watch-chains, handkerchiefs, pens and pencils and such miscellaneous bits and pieces as most people collect over the years.

Once the list was complete I was confident that I would not have to make any additions to it. It appeared to me that he was unlikely to buy any new clothes. The family motto *Let Curzon hold what Curzon held* certainly applied to his wardrobe. He even had some of his grandfather's clothes which he wore when he went shooting. The only time I recall him having anything new was when he and Lady Scarsdale were invited to a society wedding in London. Left to himself he probably would have put together an outfit from the clothes already in his wardrobe. I think it must have been Lady Scarsdale who persuaded him to have an expensive frock coat tailored for the occasion. It was a beautiful garment styled in the Victorian manner, and after his death it passed to his cousin and heir, Francis Curzon.

For the wedding Lord Scarsdale insisted on wearing with the new frock coat a favourite waistcoat of cream coloured silk charmingly embroidered with flowers. But it was very old and very much the worse for wear. When I got it out I said to him:

'You can't wear this, m'Lord.'

'Why not?' he asked.

'Well, just look at it. It's threadbare.' I held it up to the light and he could see it was almost falling to pieces.

'Leave it out all the same, Adams.'

I found another waistcoat which I packed in his suitcase but when I went back some time later I noticed he was busy sticking up the silk waistcoat with sellotape and he insisted I pack it for him. He then pulled out from his wardrobe a pair of shoes he had worn at the Jack Dempsey v Gene Tunney heavyweight fight about 40 years before. They were brown calf and white buckskin, what I believe used to be known as 'co-respondent' shoes, and anything less suitable for wearing with a frock coat to a society wedding would be hard to imagine. But, fortunately, the leather had hardened and shrunk over the years, and try as he might he could not get his feet into them.

While making the inventory I came upon two loaded revolvers partly concealed in the linen press in his bedroom. I was not surprised at the find since I knew he was obsessed with weapons of all kinds but it did cross my mind that it was extremely dangerous of him always to keep them fully loaded. I mentioned my anxiety to him on one occasion.

'Don't worry, Adams,' he said. 'There's only you and I know they are there and I'm not going to shoot you.'

That, it seemed, was the only reassurance I was going to get.

I also came across some photographs of a young Lady Scarsdale reclining in the nude, tastefully done by a professional photographer. There was no doubt she had been a very beautiful woman. I speculated that she had perhaps arranged to have the photos taken when setting her cap at an eligible lord.

I soon mastered the technique of serving at dinner parties; although these functions occurred rather too frequently for my liking. Our entertaining took place on Friday or Saturday evenings, occasionally both nights in the same week. During the shooting season there were always Tuesday and Wednesday dinner parties too for the 'guns' and their ladies, who stayed the nights preceding and following a shoot. Even a small formal dinner party added considerably to my work. Each guest would require in cutlery alone seven or eight pieces, which meant that for a party of eight I might have 64 pieces of silver flatware to clean or at least rub over before setting the table. This was apart from the serving silver, the plates, dishes and the numerous decorative items that adorned the table – not to mention the extra washing up afterwards.

Lady Scarsdale's dinner parties were always popular. She would send down to Harrods or Fortnum and Mason for delicacies which Derby could not supply: caviare, quails' eggs, pâté de foie gras and other exotic dishes associated with gracious living. She also sent away for guinea fowl, saddles of lamb and joints of beef. She always expressed dissatisfaction with the local butchers, complaining that they did not hang the meat and game long enough. The wine merchant called about once a month, usually on his way to or from Chatsworth. Lord Scarsdale kept a good cellar, although he never drank himself.

Formality was observed at all times in the dining room. The most important lady guest sat on Lord Scarsdale's right and was served first. The dishes were offered from the left-hand side of the diners. In this I found it a slight advantage in being left-handed since I could balance the serving tray on the palm of my left hand and extend it comfortably towards the guest. Had I been right-handed there could easily without care have occurred a bit of shoulder jostling resulting in the guest leaning away from the butler.

Soup was rarely served at Kedleston, but when on the menu it was the one dish which the butler serves directly onto the plates himself. I would ladle it from a large tureen on my side table and take the soup plates one by one to each guest. A more usual starter would be smoked salmon, Parma ham, prawns or salmon mousse.

The order of serving the main course was meat and gravy first, then green vegetables and then potatoes. Etiquette permitted the guests, if they wished, to start on the meat and gravy before I went round with the vegetables. When there were a large number of guests present it was a slow procedure going round on my own. On some occasions, when there were no top-drawer guests present, Lady Scarsdale herself might get up and serve the vegetables, following me round the table as I offered the meat. Eventually she suggested that perhaps Betty might like to help me at luncheon and dinner parties. This she did and we quickly made an efficient and smooth-running team. And it meant Betty did not have to sit by herself for hours in the evenings until I arrived home about midnight.

One evening I was going round refilling the wine glasses and I could not help overhearing Major Knowles holding forth about an incident at his house that week. The Major was a bluff, no-nonsense character, who may have had some decent feelings underneath his brash exterior but these were kept well hidden. He was talking about his staff, who had got themselves up into a deputation and had gathered outside the estate office. Sipping claret, Major Knowles warmed to his story.

'There they were standing around sheepishly. "What the devil is this?" I asked them. They shuffled about for a few moments and then the damned spokesman had the cheek to say they wanted a rise of 10 shillings a week. "Right," I said, "You can have your rise but you'll all take your notice at the same time and if there's any of you want to stay on, you'll come back at 10 shillings less a week." That soon put them in their place.'

He was chuckling at the way he had dealt with them. I remembered Lady Scarsdale's instruction about not taking any notice of what might be said about servants, but at times it was hard to forget such comments.

The main course was followed by pudding, a savoury or dessert (sometimes both) and then coffee. I would place the coffee tray in front of Lady Scarsdale and she would pour and pass the cups round. After this the ladies would retire and leave the gentlemen to their port and cigars. Lady Scarsdale used to whisper to me not to let them linger too long. She would tell me to go back to the dining room after 15 or 20 minutes and rattle a few dishes. Lord Scarsdale always picked up this signal and made a move to join the ladies upstairs.

It was at dinner parties, and to a lesser extent luncheon parties, that I met the 'interesting people' which Lady Scarsdale had promised would be one of the perks of my job. These meetings were, of course, only on the most superficial of levels, but as time went by I came to know and be known by close friends of the family and often on receiving them I would be greeted with a wink or a raised eyebrow and a stage whisper asking: 'Who have we tonight, Adams?' The regulars would usually go upstairs unannounced but VIPs I always preceded upstairs, entering the sitting room and announcing them formally.

The guests included friends and acquaintances of the Scarsdales from many walks of life. There were the well-to-do Derbyshire families, the titled and landed gentry of the county, foremost among whom were the Duke and Duchess of Devonshire. Then there were celebrities from the film and theatre world; businessmen; personalities of the day; professional sportsmen; Lady Scarsdale's friends from the Continental aristocracy; and on one or two occasions British royalty.

One of Lord Scarsdale's sisters was married to Sir Robert Carey, MP for Withington and at that time Father of the House. I cannot recall Lady Carey coming to Kedleston, but Sir Robert was a frequent visitor, often stopping off on his way to his constituency. He would on occasion bring one or other of his parliamentary colleagues with him. Of these the one who impressed me most was George Thomas, later Lord Tonypandy. I found him to be unassuming and natural, devoid of airs and graces. Sir Robert, too, was of similar vein. They both found time to stop and talk to me properly, not just a polite exchange of a few words. Two other visitors it was a pleasure to have in the house were Sir Philip Magnus-Allcroft and Kenneth Rose. Both were researching the life of Lord Curzon. Kenneth Rose stayed on numerous occasions whilst completing his book, eventually published in two volumes in 1969.

But what did it all add up to – apart from the fact that I had served noisettes of lamb to the Duke of Devonshire and strawberry mousse to Lady Barnet? That John Loder had shown me his worry beads made from South American gemstones or that I had pressed Godfrey Winn's trousers and polished Reresby Sitwell's boots? It gave me, I suppose, a glimpse of entirely different and privileged lives that few people would ever see. But they were not, apart from a few exceptions, lives I could respect, not lives I would want to live for all their wealth and leisure.

CHAPTER
11

At the end of my first year as butler, when I looked in my diary and totalled up the amount I had received in tips it came to £80, far short of Lady Scarsdale's predicted £200. Some of the tips were from gentlemen guests staying at the Hall for whom I acted as valet but most came from the 'guns' during the shooting season. At this rate I knew it would be far longer than five years before Betty and I had our £1,000. When I opened my first wage packet after becoming butler I found I had one pound a week more than when I was houseman. I had been expecting slightly more than this in view of my increased responsibilities and much longer working hours. Lady Scarsdale must have considered that one pound a week plus meals was a more than adequate rise. She was not to know that I ate very little of the food prepared in the kitchen, which was still far from hygienic. The mews flat was certainly an improvement on the village cottage, however. Of the other inducements Lady Scarsdale had offered me, it seemed the only one I could now look forward to was receiving a glowing reference when I left.

There was, however, one way in which I felt I could derive some benefit from my present situation, and that was to take advantage of my close proximity to the paintings, furniture and silver and make a detailed study of them. I had unrestricted access to all parts of the Hall – to the state rooms, including the Library, to the strong room and the muniments room, to the Indian Museum, not to mention the attics, cellars and outbuildings, all of which housed neglected and forgotten treasures. And I was able to handle and study everything closely.

I bought myself a pocket magnifying glass which enabled me to examine the silver and porcelain in minute detail. Sometimes I also fetched a tall step-ladder and climbed up to inspect the brush work on paintings. In the Music Room when examining Giordano's *The Triumph of Bacchus* I found myself eyeball to eyeball with a leopard and the decapitated head of a goat beneath the god's chariot. With glass in hand, too, I could make my own Grand Tour of the paintings, lingering in the Tuileries gardens, crossing the Alps to Venice, visiting the port of Naples, wandering among classical ruins and consorting with all the gods of the pantheon.

As well as the items on the inventory, both those that belonged to the Kedleston Estate and those that belonged to Lord and Lady Scarsdale personally, there were always additional items coming into the house. Lady Scarsdale used to go once a fortnight to the auction rooms of Richardson and Linnell in Derby, where sales of antique and household effects were held. There were at the time a large number of antiques coming on the market as a result of what I called 'The Dissolution of English Country House' in the 1950s and 60s.

She would go to the auction rooms on viewing day, get one of the porters to bid for her and then have her purchases delivered by van. She bought on one occasion an 18th-century cradle which she placed in the State Boudoir. She dressed the cradle with antique baby covers and I must admit that when photos of the Boudoir appeared in the guide book, the cradle looked as if it had stood there since the house was built.

My study of antiques now seemed to be paying off. Lady Scarsdale would often ask me to look at items she had purchased when they arrived in the van and give my opinion. Sometimes I would have to disillusion her. 'Your lovely old warming pans, m'Lady, are modern reproductions.' She would then be furious. She would send all the stuff back and threaten never to attend the auctions again. But she always returned, buying gifts for friends and family, stocking up on Christmas presents and bidding for paintings for her elder son, Mr Richard. He amassed these in bundles of a hundred and sold them to Americans – in the days before Victorian paintings became fashionable.

The muniments room at Kedleston was a part of the Hall I seldom entered. No one was allowed into this room except Lord and Lady Scarsdale, the agent Walters and the butler. Not that anyone would have been able to gain access easily even if they had wished. The first obstacle was a thick, steel, safe-type door set in an equally thick steel frame. The room was situated on the ground floor in one of the dampest parts of the house with the result that both door and frame were slowly sinking and twisting and it required two men with crowbars to prize the door open.

One day while I was working in the corridor nearby, Lord Scarsdale came along with the key, tried the door but could not, of course, get in. I told him he would have to wait while I went for a crowbar and some assistance. I found Tommy Brown, who was always glad of an excuse to come inside the house, and he gave me a hand. When the door was eventually opened Tommy had something to ask Lord Scarsdale.

'Excuse me, m'Lord. Could I beg a favour?'

'What do you want, Tommy?'

'Well, m'Lord, I've worked here for 40 years and I've seen and been everywhere in the house except the muniments room. Could I put my foot inside the door, just to say I've been in?'

'Of course you can, Tommy. There you are.'

Tommy put his foot over the threshold and seemed more than satisfied. He had no desire to examine the contents of the room.

Inside was an inner door with a grille, and steel shutters protected the windows. The room was surprisingly small, a mere 10ft by 10ft, much smaller than the strong room. There were shelves and cubby-holes stacked full of documents wrapped in brown paper and tied with ribbons in the manner the Victorians stored their deeds. In the centre of the room stood a table covered with metal and cardboard boxes, and more cardboard boxes were piled on the floor. But the damp had wreaked even more havoc here than in the cellars and other neglected places, and dust and cobwebs shrouded everything.

One day when I was alone inside searching for something for his lordship, Lady Scarsdale happened to pass by. She never went in the room as far as I knew but this day, noticing the door open, she came in to see what was going on and held up her hands in horror, just as she had done when she saw the state of our flat.

'Good grief! What's this, Adams? What a mess! We'll have to get this sorted out. It's a disgrace. We've had a letter from a gentleman who's coming to research the organ. If he comes in here, what on earth is he going to think?'

The organ in question stood in the Music Room. It was made by Snetzler, a German who settled in England and became one of the most famous organ builders of the 18th century. The instrument was housed in a special case designed by Robert Adam. It was an elegant piece though I never heard it played. I did once open the doors to look at the keyboard but I decided I had better not touch anything. I noticed the leather-work was rotting away and the whole thing might have been riddled with woodworm for all I knew.

Lady Scarsdale, ever impatient, wanted to make a start at once on tidying the muniments room. Surprisingly, a power point was still working, as was the single light bulb which lit the room dimly. We plugged in a small electric fire and I managed to open the steel shutters to admit a little more light and some air. Only when this was done did the full extent of the damage become apparent. I lifted one of the tin boxes from the table and the bottom fell out immediately having rusted away over the years. I began to move a number of cardboard boxes outside to the corridor thinking that I would take them to the boiler room in the cellar and dry them out. But Lady Scarsdale had other ideas.

'Take them away and burn them, Adams.'

'But shouldn't we at least try and dry some of them out, m'Lady? Or get advice from the County Archivist?'

'Get them burnt, Adams. We can't let anyone see this. If other people haven't looked after the place, why should we?'

What other people, I wondered. I hardly thought Lord Curzon had let the muniments room fall into such neglect. He had been a scholar as well as an administrator and during his last years at Kedleston had searched the archives to write a history of the church. So that left only Richard Scarsdale himself, who had lived at the Hall for the last 40 years. But Lady Scarsdale was right to the extent that some of the documents were beyond saving, almost beyond handling – just a wet, slimy mess. I threw the worst of them into the all-devouring boiler where the red-hot coke consumed them. Hundreds of documents were destroyed this way; hundreds of years of history went up in smoke. Lady Scarsdale, realising by now that the cleaning, tidying and sorting was too large a job for me to tackle in addition to my duties as butler, gave some thought as to who might help out.

The person she thought of was Keith James, a tenant living in the schoolhouse in the village. Keith James was a part-time professional actor. He played small bit parts on television and had, I believe, appeared once or twice in *Coronation Street*. At this time he was 'resting'.

Lady Scarsdale must have told him that the place needed a quick 'clean up and a tidy' and may have asked him to do it in return for repair work carried out at the schoolhouse. At all events the poor man had no idea of what he had let himself in for. When he realised the immensity of the task, he was not best pleased.

Estate workers helped out with the heavy and basic cleaning work. I spent what time I could scraping away at the bottom of the outer door with a file. If the room was to be opened every day for Keith James we obviously did not want the pantomime with the crowbars each time. Eventually when the room was ready Keith set about examining and organising the documents.

I used to go in once or twice a day to take him a coffee and keep an eye on what was happening. One section he told me he could do nothing about. This was a wall full of tiny pigeon-holes containing very early parchments written in mediaeval French. They were covered with wax seals which looked as if they would have fallen apart had anyone tried to open them. After a while Keith took to coming to the butler's pantry at the end of the day to have a wash and I would make him a cup of tea before he set off for the village. Invariably he brought some document along with him which his day's tidying had brought to light; which he had found interesting and which he thought I might like to see.

One afternoon he burst into the pantry with great excitement. 'These will interest you,' he said.

He placed on the table a number of small, rather thin and narrow notebooks, each one filled with neat but exceptionally tiny handwriting. A short examination showed them to be diaries relating to life aboard ship in the late 18th century and we soon deduced that they were the diaries of Admiral Henry Curzon. He was one of the lesser-known members of the family. Subsequent research has shown that he had a long career in the Royal Navy, entering as a midshipman in 1776 at the age of 10, receiving his commission in 1783 and eventually becoming Vice-Admiral of the Blue, and then Admiral. A portrait of him had been relegated to the attics.

The diaries covered his years of service in the East Indies. His handwriting, although minute, was beautifully executed – clear and easy to read and every page a delight to behold. The subject matter was equally fascinating. He depicted in great detail the day-to-day life on-board ship, together with his observations on the officers and crew under his command. Of particular interest to me were the punishments given for misconduct, usually in the form of lashings. As I read on certain names would appear again and again and it became clear from his remarks that that on these occasions he took no pleasure in having to enforce the rules of punishment. He did, however, take great pleasure in observing and recording the changing moods of the weather, writing descriptions of the ports visited, and the people and wildlife of the area.

Keith and I discussed these diaries at length. Seeing them from an actor's point of view, Keith suggested that in the right hands they could easily be adapted for a TV or radio series, and he toyed with idea of asking Lord Scarsdale's permission to take them to London to be examined for this possibility. In the meantime I kept the diaries locked in the butler's pantry until I had finished reading them and then I returned them to him to put back in the muniments room.

The muniments yielded one other surprise. One evening Keith was most anxious for me to go to the room with him and see his latest find. I finished washing the tea things and wondered what could be so urgent as he hurried me along the length of the Armoury Corridor and the corridor beyond, across Caesars' Hall and out into the Garden Corridor. Once in the room Keith took a large wooden box from one of the shelves and placed it on the table.

'I bet not many people know this is here,' he said.

Keith opened the box and stood awaiting my reaction. I looked down on a porcelain bowl, about the size of a punch bowl, hand-painted with a border of flowers. But what made it unique was that in the centre had been painted an erect phallus, from the end of which dangled a moneybag. I looked at it in amazement. The bowl was undoubtedly 18th century and I could only think that it had been specially commissioned for some sort of secret society, something similar perhaps to the Hell Fire Club. Had Nathaniel Curzon who built the Hall been practising strange orgiastic rites? There was a label in the box which at the time only added to the mystery rather than clarify it, merely telling us that it was a Benison Bowl.

With my commitment to looking after the house I gave no more thought to the matter of the Benison Bowl or to Admiral Henry's diaries for many years. Keith James took sick and died before completing his work in the muniments room. Much later a self-appointed archivist, Leslie Harris, came on the scene and I asked him if he had ever come across the Admiral's diaries but he denied ever having seen them. So here was a mystery. Did Keith James ever take them to London? Did someone else get their hands on them? Or did Leslie Harris himself spirit them away? He once told me that the information he had access to was very saleable in London among people who were eager for tales about families like the Curzons. The diaries have not been traced to this day and the only certain thing is that I read them and regarded them as fascinating documents of naval history.

The staff at Kedleston was forever changing. Gatekeepers, estate workers, maids, cleaners, cooks and housemen came and went continually. The names of most of these people I have long since forgotten, but one cleaner I do recall as a result of a project her daughter undertook. This young woman had taken it upon herself to write to the *News of the World* offering to correspond with any lonely or elderly person wanting a pen friend. One of the replies she received was from a woman living in Newcastle who had retired from service some years earlier and now spent her time writing and broadcasting locally. Being thus occupied she had replied not to acquire a pen friend but because the Kedleston address had caught her eye. It turned out she had worked at Kedleston Hall as a girl and in the letters which followed she described vividly her life in the house.

She had been born in the Newcastle area and as soon as she was old enough to work she had been hired by the then Lord Scarsdale (the 4th Baron Scarsdale, 1831–1916, 'Grandfather') and sent to Kedleston as a laundry maid. She described how, still a child, she had made the slow train journey from Newcastle and how she was met at Derby station by horse and trap to be taken the long and lonely road to Kedleston, and then to pass through massive and frightening iron gates. After another lengthy drive through the wooded park she had her first view of the house.

To her, as a child, the gates seemed like the entrance to a prison, and on first seeing the house she saw only a dark, forbidding place. She wrote: 'These first impressions were soon proved to be true.' She said the house was indeed a prison for her and her young companions and she described in detail the harshness and cruelty they all suffered. They not only had to do the family laundry but that of the many servants too. She told of the pecking order and the squabbles and fights which arose because of the harshness of the regime. The only comfort she and her friend found was to cuddle close at night and cry themselves to sleep. One day, old Mr Smith, the butler, was sacked when on a stormy morning he was too ill and weak to climb the stairs and walk along the parapet to hoist Lord Scarsdale's flag on the roof. The only happy memory she had was of a certain Christmas when she was given a present by one of the ladies. It was a packet of hairpins.

As each letter arrived it was passed on to me to read and eventually I gave the entire collection to Lady Scarsdale, who read them and then upon my suggestion had them put into the muniments room for safekeeping. They provided an interesting account of conditions at the Hall in Grandfather's day but enquiries have shown that, like Admiral Henry's diaries, they too seem to have disappeared.

CHAPTER
12

The position of agent, or more correctly Clerk to the Estate, carried responsibility for the management of all cottages, farms and land belonging to the Scarsdales; the letting of the parkland for grazing; collection of rents; supervision of estate and household accounts; and sundry miscellaneous duties such as the selling of timber, overseeing the branding of cattle and interviewing applicants for new appointments.

The only occupant of the post I had known to date was Mr Cyril Walters, the man who had tried to deter me from taking the job of houseman on our first visit, who had wanted to send Betty and me on our way before we had even got out of the car. Over the years I had many times speculated what course my life might have taken had I followed his advice and turned the car round and driven away. There were many occasions too when I wished I had done just that.

Walters was in his 60s when I arrived and had been at the Hall for many years. He may perhaps have managed the estate efficiently at the start but by my time he was getting hopelessly out of his depth. His problem was that he was terrified of Lord and Lady Scarsdale and was afraid to tell them anything which he knew they would not want to hear: of the deterioration of the properties and the money that needed spending on them; of the general dissatisfaction among the tenants, particularly the farmers; and of the mounting household bills which were coming in with insufficient funds to cover them.

On one occasion during my time as houseman he asked me to accompany him to the funeral of old Mr Sentence, the gardener. He was the kindly man who had given me help and advice in dealing with the trio of Labradors. I assumed that Walters had invited me to attend the funeral because he felt there would not be many mourners present. But when we reached Markeaton Crematorium I was surprised at the large turnout, particularly of tenant farmers.

After the service, as we made our way to the car park, the farmers were waiting to confront Walters and air their grievances, and for a moment I thought things were going to turn ugly. Walters managed to escape their clutches but was obviously unnerved by the incident and invited me to accompany him to a local pub where he ordered whiskies for us both.

When I was butler I overheard one or two conversations between Walters and Lord Scarsdale when Walters had plucked up enough courage to tell his lordship that bills were mounting up. Lord Scarsdale merely shrugged it all off. He told Walters to pay a bit here and there and keep the tradesmen quiet. Eventually Walters was either too scared or too ill to come in at all, and it was put about that he was now retiring.

Lady Scarsdale appeared to know nothing of Walters' neglect of the estate until letters began arriving in her personal mail demanding settlement of unpaid accounts. She went one morning with the Commodore over to the office to look at the books and she was in for a shock.

'Oh, Adams, you'll never believe it. Not a single bill has been paid for months. I'll never be able to go into Derby again. I daren't show my face there. Whatever are we going to do?'

She and the Commodore spent many days in the office working at the books trying to sort out the mess.

After Walters' departure his post was advertised and a number of smart and presentable applicants attended for interview. But the wages were far too low for any of these to be attracted to the position. Walters had once told me that his wages were only slightly higher than mine.

The man who eventually took the post was Basil Haines. He was a tall and efficient looking ex-army officer, but he seemed to have little experience of running an estate like Kedleston and was confused by it all. If he felt in any way inadequate to his duties he did not let it worry him. The cook at the time often invited him to take tea in the kitchen and he and I got on well together. In the end it was not his incompetence but a woman who brought about his downfall.

One day, quite unexpectedly, Lady Scarsdale said to me: 'Adams, I think we might be getting a man to help you. His lordship's old batman has written asking for a job. He'll make an ideal footman.'

She filled me in with some of his details saying that at one time, before the war, this Mr Hurst had done a bit of work about the house. As it happened I later saw the letter he had written. Some time previously there had been a panic when a letter containing a cheque from the Duke of Devonshire had inadvertently been thrown away and to avoid any repetition I had been instructed to look carefully at everything in the waste paper basket before it was finally disposed of. And so I had the opportunity to read Mr Hurst's letter.

He started by introducing himself and reminding Lord Scarsdale that he had lived in North Lodge for a while before the war and had then gone with him as his batman. Their paths had separated during the war but he was now wondering if there might be some possibility of employment and a cottage on the estate for himself and his wife. He'd be pleased to work in any capacity either in the house or outside etc. etc.

The result was he was taken on as footman and he and his wife were given Ireton Lodge, the third and smallest entrance to the Hall. This gateway was rarely used, except on shoot days.

I soon discovered that Lady Scarsdale's expectation of Hurst as an ideal footman was an optimistic one. There was scarcely any task I set him to do that he was capable of carrying out satisfactorily. He was much older than me, appeared rather feeble and could not get up and down stairs without difficulty. He had very bad bunions and had cut his shoes open to relieve the painful pressure these caused him. He was no use at all in the dining room, hobbling about as he did with his feet looking so unsightly. He was not much good as a valet either. When I asked him to press one of Lord Scarsdale's suits, I had to intervene quickly to stop him ruining it. In the end I just let him potter about and clean a few boots and shoes. It was easier that way.

Despite Hurst's infirmities I could feel no sympathy for him. Very quickly I realised that he was lazy, cunning, self-opinionated and deceitful. After a while he began complaining of back trouble and before the end of his first month he stopped coming to the house altogether. His last piece of advice to me was: 'Don't let them shit on you, Adams.'

No one was allowed to occupy a property on the estate without contributing something, either in rent or labour, and so his wife came in his place to work as a cleaner in the family wing.

Mrs Hurst was to cause far more trouble than her husband ever did. She was a brazen woman, scared of no one, given to speaking her mind and she interfered in everything. She was not particularly physically attractive in my opinion, although the cook who had seen a photo of her in a ball gown taken some years earlier declared her a handsome woman. Mrs Hurst told me that before coming to Kedleston she had worked in a factory where production involved the use of platinum. Quite openly she admitted that she had been taking off-cuts and pieces of scrap platinum and selling them.

'And then I got myself caught, didn't I,' she went on with some indignation, 'and got the sack.'

This disclosure told me several things about Mrs Hurst. Firstly, and obviously, she was a thief; secondly she was on the ball enough to know of a contact who would buy scrap platinum from a dubious source; and thirdly she had no shame in admitting what she had done. I began to wonder whether Mr Hurst's whole object from the start had not been to secure another job for his wife and that he had no intention of working at Kedleston himself.

It was not long before Mrs Hurst's light fingers were busy in the family wing. I noticed one day that a number of 18th-century doorstops, or door porters, were missing. These objects are of ornamental brass with a lead core and stand some 18in high. They are used to hold doors open or sometimes to keep a banging door closed. I mentioned to Mrs Hurst that the door porters had mysteriously disappeared. She had the grace to blush and the next day I was pleased to note they were back in place again.

Some time later Harold Reader, the houseman, noticed that something was going on between Mrs Hurst and Mr Haines. Harold put it to me that they were getting 'over-friendly'. It was a little more than 'Good morning Mrs Hurst' – 'Good morning Mr Haines' which was the only exchange required of them.

There were, of course, numerous hideaways for secret assignations in a place like Kedleston and Harold told me he had seen Haines and Mrs Hurst going to the Walkabout. The Walkabout was a low narrow passageway right at the top of the house running round three sides of the Marble Hall behind the curved panels which were intermediate between walls and ceiling. There were two entrances to the

Walkabout, one on the east and the other on the west side, and from it a small flight of steps gave access to the roof. It was lit by two electric light bulbs at the end of each arm of its U shape. The Walkabout was a part of the Hall totally unknown to most of the staff since they would have no reason to go there. Harold Reader knew of it because he sometimes came with me on to the roof to assist with raising or lowering the Curzon banner on the flagpole.

On an earlier occasion when I was in the Walkabout I had noticed some vertical slits in the inner wall, low down near the floor, and when I bent to peer through these I was surprised to find myself looking down not only on the Corinthian capitals of the marble columns which supported the ceiling but on the architrave above them too. Such an unusual perspective of the Marble Hall fascinated me and as far as visibility and the awkwardness of the position would allow I knelt down and twisted round to look at the three sides of the hall. At the southern end immediately over the entrance to the Saloon an unexpected example of graffiti caught my eye. Scrawled in red paint in letters about a foot high was the statement LORD SCARSDALE IS A BUGGER. This, of course, was invisible from any place but the Walkabout, and then only when one bent down to peer through the slits. It could only have been painted when scaffolding was erected. I assumed the hall must have been redecorated since it was built in the mid-18th century and I guessed that the graffiti was Victorian and referred to 'Grandfather', the Revd Arthur Curzon, fourth Baron Scarsdale, who was reputed to have been a harsh employer and landlord.

One afternoon Harold Reader had followed Haines and Mrs Hurst up to the Walkabout and in a spirit of malicious spite had locked them in. Once having trapped them, however, he was not sure what to do with them, and not wanting a confrontation with Haines he had after some time crept up again and unlocked one of the doors. On another occasion he told me he had seen them walking openly arm in arm across the park and alongside the lakes.

At this time the Commodore when he was on leave occupied a large self-contained flat at the top of the main part of the Hall. It was part of Mrs Hurst's duties to clean Cross Stitch Flat, as it was called, both when the Commodore was in residence and when he was at sea. Again it was Reader, who seemed to spend most of his time watching the movements of other staff, who reported to me that Mrs Hurst was leaving the Commodore's flat with rather more than her mop and cleaning bucket, and that he considered things were getting a bit out of hand. He told me too that Haines and Mrs Hurst spent an hour or so every afternoon in Cross Stitch flat. Mrs Hurst worked only in the mornings so she had no right to be about the house in the afternoon. By this time I found her attitude was becoming almost unbearable. She had been rude to me and rude to Betty, and although we all had a grumble about Lord and Lady Scarsdale at times she was more than insulting in the comments she passed about them. She must have felt herself quite safe, being 'in' with the agent and that no one could touch her. I decided the time had come to take action.

The following afternoon I concealed myself at a vantage point from where I could watch the entrance to the Commodore's flat, and shortly after two o'clock Mrs Hurst came along in her jaunty manner and let herself in. A little while later Haines came along, made sure the coast was clear, then he too entered Cross Stitch flat.

I sat myself down on the small flight of steps that led to the only door into the place and, distasteful though it was, I noted down the time they had gone in: 2.15pm. I waited about half an hour but no one came out. After waiting a little longer I went up the few wide stairs and tried the door. It was locked. I knocked sharply on the door and called out: 'Anyone in there?'

There was a scuffling inside and then Mrs Hurst called: 'It's me, Mr Adams. Won't be a minute. I'll be down directly.'

A few moments later she emerged, looking unusually sheepish for her, and mumbled some excuse about leaving a duster behind. I escorted her downstairs and made sure she left the building. I then returned to catch the bigger fry. I sat on the stairs again and must have waited a good half hour with not a sound coming from the flat. Eventually the door opened a fraction, then a bit wider, and Haines crept out.

'Good afternoon, Mr Haines,' I said, taking him completely by surprise. 'Don't bother creeping about. I know you've been in there with Mrs Hurst. And you've been there since' – I looked at my notebook – 'quarter past two and it's now half past three.'

Haines knew he was caught. There was no possible excuse he could give or any way of talking himself out of the situation. He immediately said how stupid he'd been, that he knew he shouldn't have done it and that he was awfully sorry.

'If you report this, I'll be fired. You know that, don't you?'

I told him I knew very well he'd be sacked. But considering that he was probably less to blame than Mrs Hurst I thought there might be a way round the situation. I told him I wouldn't report him on this occasion if he would do something for me in return. He jumped at the chance.

'Of course, of course. I'll do anything. Just tell me what it is.'

'Well, you have a word with this Mrs Hurst friend of yours and tell her that she must change her behaviour and change her attitude and treat me and Mrs Adams and the rest of the staff with the respect we deserve. If you do that and her attitude improves and there's no repetition of these goings on in the Commodore's flat, or anywhere else, then I will keep quiet about what has happened.'

Next morning Mrs Hurst came in and if anything her attitude was worse than ever. She was throwing her weight about, giving herself airs and graces, and making snide remarks about me. I knew I had not given Haines enough time to have a word with her, that I was not being fair to him, but something in me snapped. I left what I was doing and went straight upstairs. I met her ladyship in the corridor and she could see I was upset.

'Is everything all right, Adams?'

'Not really,' I said. 'I'm sorry to have to interrupt you like this but I must see his lordship.'

'Oh, can't I help?'

'No, not in this matter, m'Lady.'

'Well surely it's nothing you can't tell me. There's no need to worry his lordship.'

'I'm sorry m'Lady. I must see his lordship first and then I'll tell you afterwards.'

I knew if I told Lady Scarsdale first she would brush it aside for the sake of keeping peace and quiet in the house and for the sake of keeping her staff. I knocked on his lordship's bedroom door and went in.

Lord Scarsdale was still in bed. By this time I had worked myself into an agitated and excitable state, and my years of self-control as a butler deserted me. I plunged straight in, telling his lordship all about Mrs Hurst and Haines locking themselves in the Commodore's flat.

'And I'm telling you this,' I continued, 'not for the sake of telling tales but because this sort of thing has been going on for a long time and I am responsible for the Commodore's flat while he's away. He especially asked me to look after his things for him. No matter what you may think of Mr Hurst from years gone by – or of Mrs Hurst – that fact is neither of them can be trusted. I've always kept things to myself because Lady Scarsdale asked me to keep the peace in this house and not complain. But this time things have gone too far. Mrs Hurst's attitude to myself, my wife and the other staff, and the comments she makes about you and her ladyship are quite out of order. I promised Haines yesterday that I would say nothing about this if he talked to her. But she came in this morning and it's as if she runs the damned place. I can't take any more of it. I can't be responsible for the house with that bloody woman undermining me at every turn. I can't.'

I paused for breath after what must have been the longest speech I had ever delivered to him.

Lord Scarsdale spoke to me very quietly and calmly.

'It's all right, Adams. Don't upset yourself so. Sit down here on the bed and calm yourself.'

I sat down on the edge of the four-poster and Lord Scarsdale continued: 'I know all about Mr Haines and Mrs Hurst. I warned Haines of what would happen if he continued with this foolishness and Mr Haines will now go and so will Mrs Hurst. You've done very well, Adams, and if we were in the army I'd have you promoted to sergeant immediately. Now, when you've recovered go downstairs and continue with your duties.'

With this two-edged compliment ringing in my ears I went downstairs. Mrs Hurst was still there, prancing about and lording it as if she were queen of the castle. Then her ladyship's maid came along with a message for her.

'His lordship wants to see you in the schoolroom, Mrs Hurst. You're to go there at once.'

Later that morning I was in the butler's pantry polishing silver when Lady Scarsdale came in.

'Oh dear, Adams, this is a mess we've got into.'

'Well, it's none of my doing m'Lady. Mrs Hurst has been upsetting the whole house since she came here. She had no right to be in the Commodore's flat.'

'Well, his lordship has sacked her and he's sacked Mr Haines too. They're both to go.' She paused for a moment. 'But there is just one thing that worries me.'

As soon as she said that I knew all was lost, that she had thought up some excuse for keeping Mrs Hurst on.

'Mr Hurst has a very violent temper,' continued Lady Scarsdale, 'and I'm rather afraid he might do Mrs Hurst some harm if all this comes out. We wouldn't want that to happen. Haines has to go but do you think, Adams, if we took Mrs Hurst away from the family wing and put her to work in the state rooms where you wouldn't run into her so often, you could agree to her staying on those terms?'

It was on the tip of my tongue to say that there would be even more opportunity for her to steal if left at large in the state rooms, but I had no proof so I kept silent. I had to agree.

So half an hour after being dismissed Mrs Hurst was reinstated. Haines' dismissal stood. The women had won the day. Lord Scarsdale, Haines and myself had all to a greater or lesser degree come off worse in this sordid episode. Haines was sacked; Lord Scarsdale was over-ruled; I was forced into compromise. We had to bow to her ladyship's wishes.

CHAPTER 13

During Haines' brief tenure of office we were for a time without a cook. And then Miss Wilson arrived. Lady Scarsdale said: 'We've got a new cook coming, Adams, and we've got to try and keep this one. Look after her, won't you. Make sure she settles in all right. See that she feels at home. Do your best to make a fuss of her.'

I realised by now that the cook's feelings received far more consideration than mine. The cook was allowed to throw tantrums, serve up indifferent meals, take days off when she felt like it, and a blind eye was turned. But I was expected to be above all that. It was taken for granted that my behaviour would be impeccable and that any personal feelings I might have would be kept well hidden.

Again I saw the taxi coming up the drive. I was in one of the state rooms at the time and watched with interest as the new cook made her first appearance. My immediate reaction was: 'Oh my God! Look at the sergeant major.'

I saw a short, stout woman, enveloped in a fur coat, but very upright in posture with chin pulled in, ordering the taxi driver about as he unloaded her luggage. There was no indication that Miss Wilson found Kedleston overwhelming. She swaggered up to the door as if she owned the place. There'll be trouble with this one, I thought.

I cannot say I got on well with her at all. Remembering what Lady Scarsdale had said I tried to be sociable by taking my meals with her and Mrs Gowan in the kitchen. Normally I ate alone in the butler's pantry. One of the first things I observed was that Cookie Wilson prepared vast quantities of food for each meal, far more than Lord and Lady Scarsdale or even the rest of us could ever eat. In the kitchen she would pile her own plate high and then pile another helping so high on Mrs Gowan's plate that it would overflow on to the table, and the two of them sat side by side devouring every last scrap. They got on well together. But it was more than I could do, to sit there watching these two gluttons gorging themselves. After a few days I made my excuses and took my meals on my own again.

Cookie Wilson was a good meat and gravy cook but rather poor with puddings, pastry and cakes. Lady Scarsdale said everything was lovely, of course. She was still frightened of losing her. There were certain rules of etiquette about what was served and when. Carrots, for example, were never served at dinner. No tinned food was eaten, with the exception of caviar and pâté de foie gras. Casseroles and stews were served only at lunchtime and roasts and grills for dinner. Into this regime Cookie Wilson introduced certain proletarian dishes, on one occasion serving up tripe and onions, and on another giving Lord Scarsdale black pudding for his breakfast. It was Cookie Wilson too who introduced them to foreign food: spaghetti. Her method of cooking it was to plunge it into boiling water and then out again so that it was tough and tasteless and scarcely edible. Lord Scarsdale detested it and my portion whenever I received any went straight into the bin.

Once Cookie Wilson had settled herself in she started to talk. She was one of those people who have been everywhere, done everything and knew everyone. She gave the impression of being acquainted with every single person in *Burke's Peerage* and of having worked for a good many of them. Had anyone mentioned their grandfather's third cousin twice removed she would have known that person. Eventually this got too much for me. I said to Haines, who sometimes took tea with us in the kitchen: 'I'm going to catch that woman out. I'm going to mention a name and I know very well she'll know nothing about him because he doesn't exist. We'll set the trap at tea-time and see how she reacts.'

As soon as she started on her bragging, I dropped the name Baron Graham into the conversation. The *Baron Graham* was one of the ships I had served on during the war. Most of the Hogarth line ships were prefixed with the name Baron but the word had no significance as a title.

'Oh, Baron Graham. Yes, a wonderful person. I worked for him before I went to the Gubbies. He has a wonderful household.'

And so she went on. Haines and I were looking at each other scarcely able to keep a straight face.

When Cookie Wilson got onto her wartime experiences she said she had been a sergeant in the WRAF. (Well done Adams, I thought, to recognise a sergeant at 20 paces.) She had had a pilot boyfriend who had been killed – in heroic and dramatic circumstances, of course. She said she was so popular on the airbase that the pilot officers used to take her up flying over London, quite frequently, to look at the bomb damage. She was also privy to all sorts of secret information.

She had not been at Kedleston long before she made it her business to go into Derby on Tuesday and Friday mornings with Lady Scarsdale and order the provisions herself. She picked out what she wanted at the County Stores and had it loaded in the Land Rover while Lady Scarsdale went to the bank, or the auction rooms, or did her personal shopping. I soon realised, since I had to help unload the Land Rover, that there were vast quantities of non-perishable provisions coming into the house. She was returning with cases of wine, tins of ham and pressed tongue, meat pastes, tins of soup, Dundee cakes, jams and mixed biscuits, all of which went into her storeroom and very few, as far as I could see, appeared on the table. Cookie Wilson told everyone she was a diabetic and as such had to be continually eating or she would go into a coma. I noticed that with her type of diabetes she seemed able to eat anything, and every meal she cooked was enough for 10 people. I began to wonder what as going on.

Cookie Wilson and I each had four days off at the end of every four weeks. (For reasons later to be explained I never managed more than two completely free days.) Rather then have us stagger these days off it suited Lord and Lady Scarsdale for us to take them at the same time and they would go to their club in London for a few days. Cookie Wilson always went to Newcastle for her time off as she had family in Consett. She left about six o'clock on the evening prior to her first day off. To start with Cookie Wilson used to get a taxi to the station, but after a while she arranged for the postman to take her in his car. She had become friendly with the postman whom she often invited in for a cup of tea about five o'clock at the end of his afternoon rounds. He made a small charge for running her to the station but it worked out cheaper than a taxi. It was the postman who inadvertently let slip what was going on.

One evening while he was waiting for Cookie Wilson to collect her belongings he said to me: 'I think I shall have to charge her extra, what with all the boxes and cases she takes with her. She'll break my springs one of these days.'

He also told me that the porters at Derby station had got so used to her and all her boxes that they would disappear when Cookie Wilson approached. One day at the station she had dropped one of her boxes as she was struggling on her own and it had smashed and there were pools of wine spreading over the platform. I had no idea this had been going on and so the next time she went off on one of her breaks I made it my business to watch and sure enough she had about half a dozen large packing cases all tied up and sealed, which she had brought from the store cupboard and loaded into the postman's car. I calculated that she was taking more than enough food to feed her family from one visit to the next. Then I remembered she had told me she had a sister who ran a small boarding house in Newcastle. Everything was falling into place. The enormous quantities of food she cooked for Lord and Lady Scarsdale were a cover-up for the amount spent on provisions. All these were bought on account and the bills sent to the office where the agent was responsible for paying them. It was obvious that Lady Scarsdale did not keep tabs on the housekeeping budget. No doubt she considered she paid the agent to do that.

I faced a dilemma. Should I report Cookie Wilson or not? I knew Lady Scarsdale was still desperately anxious to keep this woman whatever her failings, and should Cookie Wilson deny my allegations an awkward situation would arise. Neither did I wish to involve the postman and get him into trouble. I decided to make sure Cookie Wilson knew I was aware of what was going on, and hope that this would stop her activities. At the same time I thought I would try and get her on another failing which was obvious for all to see: her lack of cleanliness in the kitchen.

I was aided in this move by an unexpected development. Betty and I returned from a short holiday to find a distraught Lady Scarsdale waiting for us.

'Oh, Adams, thank God you're back. His lordship is very ill.'

At first I didn't take much notice because I knew Lord Scarsdale was inclined to go sick when it suited him. If he was sulking about something, or there was a function he did not want to attend, he would go sick. But when I saw him lying helpless on his bed I knew immediately there was something seriously wrong. Lady Scarsdale told me he had been violently sick and had stomach pains and that the doctors had been unable to make a diagnosis. I thought I knew what the trouble was.

'Have you considered it might be food poisoning, m'Lady?'

Lady Scarsdale dismissed this as nonsense, saying she had eaten exactly the same meals as his lordship and had suffered no ill effects.

'All the same,' I went on, 'I advise you to take a look at your kitchen. I'm entitled to have all my meals here but Mrs Adams prepares most of my food at home. Benny eats more in this house than I do.'

'What do you mean? Why don't you eat here?'

'Because the whole kitchen's disgusting. That's why Miss MacDonald didn't stay. The plates you eat off are clean because I wash them myself. But everything else is filthy. Go down to the kitchen when there's no one about and take a look at the place. Pull out a few drawers. Have a look at the floor. It hasn't been scrubbed for months and Mrs Gowan goes about with filthy legs and feet. You don't have to look far to see grease and flies everywhere. That's why I think his lordship must have picked up a germ which doesn't seem to have affected you.'

Some time later she took my advice and inspected the kitchen and had to agree with me.

'You're right, Adams. I'll get on to Mrs Gowan.'

'It's no use getting on to Mrs Gowan, m'Lady. It's the cook who's at fault here.'

Lady Scarsdale's method of dealing with situation was a subtle one, so subtle that it went completely over the head of Mrs Gowan and everyone else for that matter. She went upstairs to her room, sorted out half a dozen pairs of shoes, put them in a box and went down to the kitchen.

'Ah, Mrs Gowan. I've a little present for you. Just try these on for size.'

And that was it. Nothing said. She hadn't even the nerve to suggest: 'Perhaps you'd better get your feet washed and the kitchen floor scrubbed before you wear my beautiful shoes,' which was the interpretation I put upon her gift.

Lord Scarsdale made a slow recovery and we carried on in much the same way as before. Eventually Cookie Wilson left of her own accord. Her excuse was ill-health – her diabetes. As far as I could see she was still producing enormous meals and still had a healthy appetite until the day she left. Other cooks followed, in one instance a chef who 'borrowed' my game scissors to carry out running repairs on his car. But fortunately there were none who caused quite the problems that Cookie Wilson and Mad Mac had brought with them.

CHAPTER
14

It was always a relief to me when Lord and Lady Scarsdale went away on holiday and my duties, if not my responsibilities, became lighter. My own holiday (two weeks a year and no Bank Holidays) had to be taken when it suited the Scarsdales and this was usually early October, after the Hall closed to the public and before the shooting season began.

The Scarsdales had a liking for sea travel and often took a winter cruise on a cargo vessel, or sometimes they sailed to the Norwegian fjords where Lord Scarsdale would fish. Towards the end of 1965 they were planning an extended trip to the Far East. The idea was to travel out by sea on the MS *Bayernstein*, a German ship, and visit India, Malaya, Hong Kong, fly on to Japan and then return home by air some three months later.

Before they left Lady Scarsdale gave me a list of instructions and more than enough tasks to keep me busy. She wanted the ceiling of the Tapestry Corridor painted, the interior of the Fishing Lodge painted, the sequoia dining table restored, the dining room curtains taken down and sent for cleaning and a set of eight chairs recaned. It was a lot to do but I gave myself the luxury of working from nine till five and taking Saturdays and Sundays off – almost a holiday for me too.

I began with the curtains. I sat myself down in the dining room and with drawing book and pencil in hand I began sketching the curtains, showing how the pleats were arranged and how the folds fell so that they could be rehung in exactly the same way.

Lady Scarsdale also asked Betty and me to look after Benny, her pit bull terrier. This we agreed to and had him with us in the flat, considering ourselves lucky that Tango, Tarquin and Thunder had been sent to the head gamekeeper for the duration. The main problem with Benny was not his ferocity but the fact that he had never been house-trained. Lady Scarsdale would take him for long walks in the park before lunch but immediately he came back into the house he would cock his leg up any one or more of his favourite calling spots: sometimes the central column of the dining table (hence the need of restoration), or up the dining room curtains which were a pale green colour but had a yellow stain gradually creeping up from the hem. I was surprised the place did not smell. If it did I never noticed it but perhaps I had become used to it being in the dining room every day for several hours or so. Benny also used the antique display cabinets on the first floor landing, and the four-poster in his lordship's bedroom, and the curtains in the sitting room.

We had no problems with Benny in our flat. He settled in and appeared quite content. Not once did we have to mop up. He was company for Betty who used to take him out everyday up the Long Walk, a wooded footpath leading away from the west of the formal gardens behind the orangery, where there were squirrels and badger sets and all sorts of doggy attractions. In the evenings Benny liked to stretch out in front of the log fire in our sitting room.

After the curtains had been taken away I set to work on the dining table. I needed the estate men to help me lift it down to the gunroom, part of which I could use as a workshop. I had learnt about furniture restoration from my father. I now rubbed down the central column, then restained and polished it. I used beeswax polish which produces a wonderful finish if used correctly. A very small quantity of beeswax (too much produces a greasy film difficult to remove) and a lot of hard rubbing is the secret. I recaned the chairs, a slow and tedious job, requiring great attention to detail. I have never understood how the blind are supposedly able to master this skill.

One morning I took Benny out early and in the stable yard we came upon the milkman. There was a longstanding hostility between Benny and the milkman, and Benny immediately went for his ankles. The milkman beat a hasty retreat, started up his milk float and raced off down the drive towards the Village Lodge. We must have made a strange sight; the milk float hurtling towards the gate as fast as a milk float can go, Benny following in hot pursuit and me bringing up the rear on my bicycle.

The milkman reached the gates safely but when I arrived I found Benny collapsed on the ground nearby, shaking all over. He was far too heavy for me to carry back to the flat so I raced back on my bike and came down in the Land Rover to fetch him. A tenant helped me carry him upstairs and I laid him on the rug in front of the fire. After about 15 minutes or so he seemed to recover. Indeed, the next day he was back to his normal self.

Lord Scarsdale had given me a list of their ports of call and asked me to write to him to let him know how things were at the Hall. In my letter to Port Swettenham in Malaya I filled him in on the news: a picture had fallen down in the State Boudoir but sustained no damage, some of the staff were off with flu and Benny had suffered a little turn. Not long after I received letter from his lordship. It began:

Port Swettenham
Malay.
On board MS Bayernstein

Dear Adams,

This I write at Port Swettenham, the port for Kuala Lumpur, 25 miles inland, a very fine city full of magnificent buildings of strange shape and architecture but with very well kept gardens private and public and with two or three pleasant lakes tho of yellow water. The mountains inland, beyond Kuala Lumpur, are very impressive and are called the Cameron Highlands. In Penang, which we liked immensely, we took the funicular railway up to 2,700 feet and had splendid views.

He went on to say how they had visited the Zoo about five miles further on found it shut but had managed to gain admittance. (Pulled rank, I imagine.) They had seen three Sumatran tigers and taken photographs of a black gibbon monkey, some birds and a crocodile. They had then had a splendid lunch at the Salingen Club. He went on:

> This is an air-conditioned ship, thank God. How pleased am I to get back to her.
>
> Thank you very much for your splendid letter. I do hope that by now all are fit again. How lucky about the picture. I think it is of James II – these chains are impossibly weak. Before leaving I doubled them in the sitting room. I think little Benny Boy gets a cramp for a few minutes after running too fast after a motor car. I do not think it is anything else and no doubt the pursuit of the milk float to the village caused this. I hope he does not do this again for I fear for him straining his heart. I trust that Mrs Adams is well. Her ladyship says give her Benny Boy a big kiss from her.
>
> Yours,
>
> Scarsdale

The following Saturday morning I was relaxing in our first-floor sitting room and Benny was warming his tummy by the hearth when he suddenly he jumped up and ran towards the big window overlooking the stable area below. I went to see what had alerted Benny. Had he heard a voice or footsteps, I wondered. I noticed Mrs Scaife, a tenant from the flat opposite ours, walking in the yard towards her car. It so happened she was wearing a short fur coat which bore a strong resemblance to one of her ladyship's coats. Benny, still frantic with excitement, must have thought his beloved mistress was back. Even as I reached this conclusion, Benny took a flying leap at the window, went clean through and landed on the cobbles some 20ft below. Heart pounding I raced downstairs and out through the door, dreading what I was going to find. But he was still alive; still breathing, though in deep shock. Together the gardener and I carried him upstairs to the flat and I kept him warm in a blanket while Betty phoned for the vet.

After a careful examination the vet declared there were no bones broken and as far as he could tell no internal injuries. He explained to us that bull terriers were bred as fighters and were immensely strong. He advised keeping Benny quiet and resting for a few days.

Three days later Betty and I sat round the fire in the evening with Benny stretched out on the rug before us. Suddenly he gave a little sigh, his head dropped and he died peacefully there in front of us.

Once again we called the vet, although we knew there was nothing he could do. He said that without a post mortem it was difficult to determine the cause of death but in his opinion it was probably heart failure, not necessarily associated with the fall from the window.

Next day I wrapped Benny in a blanket and dug a grave for him at the back of the house in an area to the left of the Adam staircase, where a number of small plaques marked the resting place of other family dogs. Then I wrote again to Lord Scarsdale, explaining what had happened and leaving him to break the news to her ladyship.

The weeks passed by. It was now late March and all my tasks were completed. I was dreading the return of Lord and Lady Scarsdale and the questions about Benny which would inevitably follow. But when they arrived nothing was said. Lady Scarsdale made no mention of the matter. I do no even know whether she went to look at the spot where Benny was buried. His name was never mentioned again.

CHAPTER
15

Occasionally, when the spirit moved her, Lady Scarsdale would take it upon herself to organise some charitable function or a village event perhaps, or a staff outing. These occasions were few and far between and marked by Lady Scarsdale's idiosyncratic touch.

'I've had an idea, Adams,' she said one morning, as I set her breakfast tray on her lap. 'We'll have a competition for the best garden in the village and we'll give the prize to Mrs Furniss.'

Mrs Furniss was Lady Scarsdale's personal maid. She lived at Yew Tree cottage, opposite The Old Rectory on the sharp bend in the lane. Her large front garden was surrounded by a privet hedge and the view from the gate showed only a dreary concrete path leading in a dead straight line to the front door. An arch sparsely entwined with a rambling rose spanned the path, while yew trees and tall ancient conifers cast their shadow over a patchy lawn. No one would call it a prize-winning garden.

The villagers, as far as I knew, received no notification of the forthcoming competition. For decades their gardens had been used for vegetable growing to feed large families and any goodness was long since leached from the soil. And there appeared to be no keen amateur gardeners among them.

Lady Scarsdale took the Land Rover one afternoon and drove through the village as far as the last cottage looking at patches of nettles, maggoty cabbages, abandoned chicken runs and asbestos sheds. In comparison, Mrs Furniss's garden did perhaps have some merit.

Mrs Furniss duly received her prize: a Qualcast lawnmower from the factory in Derby. The enterprise was, I believe, Lady Scarsdale's roundabout attempt to cheer up a recently widowed woman.

A few months later Lady Scarsdale received a letter from Derby Cathedral requesting donations for urgently needed restoration work. Lady Scarsdale was a Catholic but this did not deter her from throwing herself wholeheartedly into a scheme to raise funds for the Anglican cathedral.

She decided she would hold a sale of antiques. She began by writing letters to all her wealthy and influential friends in the county inviting them to donate items for the sale. The response was good. Very soon porcelain, glassware, jewellery and even carpets began arriving and these were stored in Caesars' Hall. Among the items was a small silver cigarette case with the look of Fabergé about it. It wasn't Fabergé, of course; the hallmark was an English one. But it was a splendid piece with a gilt lining and Lady Scarsdale bought it for herself. There was a claret jug which her son had, together with a set of six liqueur glasses in the form of thistles. The most unusual item was an 18th-century actor's mirror for a theatre dressing room. It was a free-standing piece and consisted of a turned mahogany column on tripod feet. Fitted to the column, in addition to the mirror, was a tray for bottles and jars, and a pair of adjustable candlesticks.

To provide even more items Lady Scarsdale went to the strong room and brought out a few pieces of her own silver and asked me to assist her in turning out cupboards and storerooms in search of other treasures. The cupboard at the bottom of the back stairs yielded a particularly good haul. Out came blue-and-white meat dishes, wine and spirit decanters of all shapes and sizes, candlesticks, oriental porcelain and a stack of old prints. I had a packet of labels ready and as Lady Scarsdale called out the prices I stuck the labels on: sixpence here, a shilling there, and occasionally two and sixpence for a special piece. I asked her if I might buy one or two items.

'Of course, Adams,' she said. 'Just hand the money in at the office.'

I picked out half a dozen blue-and-white meat dishes at sixpence each. They were massive chargers with transfer-printed decoration and runnels for the gravy. I realised later that what I should have taken was a piece of yellow-and-green Chinese porcelain. It was a small bowl of the 'famille jaune' type, broken in two and so appearing worthless. I know now that even after restoration it would have been worth a small fortune. I do not know what happened to it. I imagine it was thrown away at some time.

Lady Scarsdale invited Arthur Negus, an up-and-coming celebrity in the antiques world, to open the sale. But the results were disappointing. Many items remained unsold, among them the actor's make-up stand. People probably did not realise the potential value of the pieces. It was before antique collecting began to take off; before the days of antiques fairs and television programmes devoted to the subject. All the unsold items Lady Scarsdale eventually sent to auction, where they raised a little more for the Cathedral fund.

The one and only staff outing I went on was one I would prefer to forget. Lady Scarsdale decided she was going to take the cook and me, and anyone else who wanted to go, to Chatsworth to the Horse Trials. When the day came, the cook and I left everything set out ready for dinner. I changed into mufti, and immediately after lunch, together with Mrs Furniss and one or two others, climbed into the Land Rover with Lord and Lady Scarsdale. This was to be an informal visit to Chatsworth. The Scarsdales had not told the Duke and Duchess of Devonshire of the intended trip and did not expect to be received by them.

On arrival we tumbled out of the vehicle and went our separate ways, enjoying seeing the horses put through their paces. Suddenly, about mid-afternoon, Lady Scarsdale's deep voice boomed out: 'Everyone back to the Land Rover!' And then to me: 'Round them all up, Adams. Get them here quickly. His lordship wants his tea.'

Tea, as I explained earlier, was Lord Scarsdale's favourite meal and to miss it usually put him in a bad mood for the rest of the day. I managed to gather the staff together, we climbed into the Land Rover, and then the nightmare began.

If ever a man should have been prosecuted for dangerous driving, it was Lord Scarsdale that afternoon. Fearful of being late back for tea, he gripped the steering wheel, clenched his teeth, put his foot down to the floor and drove like a maniac. Off we sped, across Chatsworth Park, hurtling over the cattle grid, shooting across a narrow bridge and off down narrow winding lanes.

Pandemonium broke out inside the vehicle. The women were screaming and trying to cling on as we were thrown from one side to the other. I was half standing and clutching at a metal strut on the roof of the vehicle. Lady Scarsdale, in the front seat, was shouting at his lordship to slow down, telling him he was completely out of his senses. Lord Scarsdale was impervious to it all, hell bent on getting back to Kedleston for his tea. The vehicle was one of the older Land Rovers with a soft canvas top and little means of seeing out for those in the back so we had no idea where we were, whether we were on roads or being jolted across fields. All I knew was we expected the Land Rover to crash or overturn at any moment.

Of course, when we got back, miraculously without accident, there was no tea ready and no one in a fit state to prepare any. Mrs Furniss was sick on the drive; the cook was a grey colour and she too was violently sick; Lady Scarsdale ran off to her bedroom and Lord Scarsdale was in a flaming temper.

At this point, I suppose, the perfect butler would have rallied round, prepared and served tea, calmed the ladies and dryly complimented his lordship on his driving. But I was as helpless as the rest. My legs were shaking. I could not stand up properly and I imagine I was as white as a sheet. For once my composure failed me.

CHAPTER 16

Lord Scarsdale's contribution to the family tree was fathering four daughters: Anne, Gloria, Juliana and Diana. As often happens with families, the four sisters were of widely differing personalities.

Anne's visits to the Hall were infrequent. I can recall only three occasions when she came to Kedleston. The first was when she and her husband moved from southern Ireland to farm on the fells and they stopped off en route. The second occasion was for the wedding of her daughter, who was married in the small church adjoining the house; and the third for her father's funeral. Whenever her name cropped up in conversation she was always referred to as 'poor Anne' for reasons I never quite understood. She appeared to me to be a naturally quiet and unassuming person.

Gloria was a tall, good-looking woman who dressed well and carried herself well. She had married a businessman, Mr Jack Bearman, and they lived for tax reasons on Jersey. They used to visit two or three times each year and once a year Gloria would come on her own, always after stag hunting with the Somerset and Devon hounds. On these occasions she would arrive with her car crammed full of suitcases and bringing her heavy riding gear with her. She had obviously married well and was quite happy to show it.

Her husband, in contrast to her stature, was small and slim and exhibited the traits of a shrewd and careful man. Whenever he visited he always wore the same already old-fashioned suit which shone from years of bad pressing. His shoes would be wrapped in newspaper instead of being packed in shoe bags, and his shaving gear and toiletries would also be wrapped in newspaper. Although the two were so very different, I felt they were deeply attached to one another. Some time later Gloria had a fall from her horse while hunting. She broke her collarbone and developed a brain tumour and died. Bearman had never seemed happy at Kedleston – I wondered whether perhaps he did not care much for Lady Scarsdale – and after his wife's death he did not visit again.

Miss Juliana was the odd one out of the four girls. The older folk about the estate had many stories to tell of her wild and mis-spent youth. All I knew for certain was that by my time she was on her third marriage and had several children from each marriage. Talk of her excesses I believe arose from her behaviour at hunt balls, which at one time used to be held regularly at Kedleston. I had some experience of hunt balls during my banding days and had witnessed many examples of wild behaviour, so I was glad these functions were no longer held at the Hall.

Miss Diana, the youngest daughter, was popular with everyone. She was a happy, cheerful young woman, demanding little attention. She had made her home in Spain where she taught English. Twice a year, at Christmas and Easter, she would come and stay about a month with us. I was always pleased to see her for she would bring cheer into our lives, especially when the Commodore was not there and Lady Scarsdale was miserable and difficult. Her staying meant taking breakfast up to her room each morning and cleaning her shoes, but these little extras were well rewarded by her presence among us. There was talk at one time that Diana was considering marriage to a member of the Spanish royal family. It was also rumoured that she had had a child in Spain. Whether there was any truth in these whispers I do not know. She did on one occasion introduce to the family an obviously well bred and distinguished looking Spanish gentleman. He stayed a few days with us but since Diana always displayed a loving attitude towards everyone it was not possible to determine whether her feelings for him ran deeper. At all events nothing came of the relationship. Diana continued her visits to Kedleston until her father died and the new lord succeeded to the title.

The mother of these four girls I never met, although Lord Scarsdale used to visit her when he went to London. He seemed to be fond of her still and often he would take a small gift with him which he would ask me to wrap. It might be a scarf or a pair of gloves. When Mildred died her funeral was conducted at Kedleston amid great pomp. Wreaths larger than I had ever seen before began arriving, each one of which had to be carried by two men between them. On the day itself more Rolls-Royces than I had ever seen were parked on the forecourt of the north front. The story was that Mildred had run off with an American millionaire and had become a very wealthy woman, but she left no will and none of her daughters inherited any of his wealth. This caused great consternation to the Scarsdales and prompted her ladyship to remark to me: 'Adams, make sure you give all your money away to your children before you die, otherwise they won't get anything. The poor girls have nothing.'

The one relative of Lord Scarsdale whose impending visits always struck panic into Lady Scarsdale was his sister, Mrs Simpson Pedlar. Magdalene Simpson Pedlar, or Marnie as she was called by the family, was some years older than Lord Scarsdale. She had been married thee times and her third husband was a shy and retiring QC. But if he were shy and retiring by nature, Marnie was just the opposite, and notice of her annual visit to Kedleston always threw the whole household into a state of anxiety and, in my opinion, unnecessary trepidation. This atmosphere would be brought about entirely by Lady Scarsdale who for reasons known only to herself would demonstrate a complete change of character. The only time I knew her to lose her self-assurance was when Mrs Simpson Pedlar was about to visit.

The lady certainly showed a domineering character to anyone willing to be bullied by her. I felt sorry for her thinking how few real friends she must have. I felt even more sorry for her husband, who was plainly browbeaten. He told me how she would often banish him to the loft in their London house where the pigeons had made homes for themselves.

During her last years when she fell ill she was asked to leave numerous private hospitals in London where her behaviour could not be tolerated. She had a niece who was a nurse in a South Wales hospital and she insisted on being sent there. But they too refused to keep her and she came to end her days with the nuns of St Mary's Nursing Home at Ednaston, about five miles from Kedleston. This was too close for comfort, however, and she made life unbearable for us all. She would be on the phone continually, asking the most silly questions. Since his lordship never answered the phone it was Lady Scarsdale who was on the end of all these annoying calls, and eventually she asked me to take every phone call when I was in the house.

They also asked me to deputise for them and visit Mrs Simpson Pedlar in the nursing home. The only time I could find to fit these visits into my routine was during my two hours off in the afternoon. So twice a week I would take the Land Rover and drive over to Ednaston. The usual opening to my visits would be: 'Oh, it's you, Adams. Well sit down here beside me and tell me everything that's been happening. I want to know everything.'

The telling would amount to no more than simply answering a barrage of questions and listening to her reminiscences. The nuns showed great patience with her. Quite often she would be violent towards them when they were trying to make her more comfortable. She and I got on fairly well together, no doubt because I was not 'family'.

One day his lordship brought her over to Kedleston for lunch. The nuns had given her the use of a wheelchair and between us, and not without some difficulty, we carried her in this up to the sitting room. Lord Curzon had planned to install two lifts in the Hall. He had undertaken a major programme of modernisation but the lift intended for the family wing which was to operate from the cellars up to the guest bedrooms on the second floor had not been installed, and after his death it had been considered too costly a project to pursue.

When lunch was ready I helped carry Marnie down again and wheeled her into the dining room to her place at the table. I had just set out the hot plates when she announced that she needed to go to the toilet. I gathered up the plates, put them back on my serving table and wheeled her along to the staff facilities on the ground floor. She said she would manage from there and would call out when ready to go back. But she found herself unable to manoeuvre her chair into the cubicle. After a short struggle and some unladylike cursing she asked for my help. I had no sooner put my hand to the chair than it suddenly tipped forward, ejecting Mrs Simpson Pedlar out and on to the floor. I must have been a little impatient and hasty and had unintentionally pressed the button which tipped the seat up. But she seemed to have come to no harm and eventually I got her back to the dining room and served lunch.

On one of my visits to the nursing home she said: 'Adams, they tell me I'm dying. Well if that is so, then it is heaven. It is wonderful.'

Whatever her faults she was, I thought, a brave woman in the face of death. When she died shortly afterwards she was cremated and her ashes were scattered across the park at Kedleston.

In great contrast to Mrs Simpson Pedlar was the Countess Orsicz whom I assumed to be a relative of Lady Scarsdale, although she may have been an old family friend. She was very much a lady of the European aristocracy of the 20s, well accustomed to good living. She had a gracious and charming manner, putting everyone at their ease. She must have been in her 60s at the time I was at Kedleston and inclined to be slow in her movements.

One evening she was late coming down to dinner and I was sent upstairs to ascertain whether all was well. She was not in her bedroom so I called out and knocked on her bathroom door. My practice of 'knock and enter' did not apply to the privacy of ladies' bathrooms, but when I heard a faint cry from within I at once opened the door and was surprised to see her lying in the bath unable to move. She told me her hip was giving her trouble and that she could not get out of the bath and would I be so kind as to assist her. I gathered up a towel to put round her, helped her to her feet and managed to get her out. Except for being cold – she must have been lying there for some time – she assured me she would be all right and would be down shortly. Not wanting to worry or embarrass them in any way, she told me to say that she had dozed off for longer than intended and to ask if she might be excused the first course.

The one family member I took more than a passing interest in was the Honourable Francis Curzon, Lord Scarsdale's cousin and heir, since I knew that if I should still be at the Hall when his lordship died then Francis Curzon would be my next employer.

CHAPTER
17

Over the years I had been witness to a succession of people who took advantage of the Scarsdales. They ranged from Mrs Hurst's almost open stealing to Cookie Wilson, who stockpiled groceries to take to her sister's boarding house up north. At first these things worried me since I was responsible for the contents of the house. But after a while I thought if my employers had so little regard for the treasures they had inherited why should I concern myself over it all. The one who outdid all the others was Otto. He did more than overstep the mark; he leapt beyond it.

Mr Otto was not on the permanent staff but was a self-employed antiques dealer, who was hired as a restorer when occasion demanded. He had been at the Hall on and off since my days as houseman. Tommy Brown had soon got the measure of Mr Otto. He could not stand the man. 'Don't take your eyes off him,' he advised me. 'Follow him everywhere. I wouldn't trust him an inch.'

Otto was German, a little older than myself and had been a member of Hitler's SS. He told me this himself. He had been taken prisoner during the war and sent to live and work on a farm in the Midlands. After the war he married the farmer's daughter, and it was perhaps his father-in-law who helped set him up in a small antiques shop in Derby. He was hardly what you would call a good-looking man, with a thin face, high cheekbones and a sallow complexion. What women saw in him I found hard to imagine, but he had certainly wormed his way into Lady Scarsdale's good books and several other leading families in the county.

The Apple Chamber was a first-floor room in the stables block, adjoining but at right angles to our flat and with a connecting door between the two. At one time it had obviously been used for storing fruit. I had discovered the remains of an orchard in a distant corner of the garden close to where tennis courts had later been laid out. By my time the trees were ancient and had been neglected for years. I sometimes gathered a few apples in late summer but there were perhaps no more than two or three trees that yielded edible fruit. Evidence now pointed to the Apple Chamber having been used as a storeroom for 50 years or more. It was crammed with surplus furniture, picture frames and all sorts of bric-a-brac. I would go in occasionally to open the windows and air the room. Much of the stuff was in poor condition but the place was a veritable treasure house for someone like Otto.

One of the first tasks Lady Scarsdale assigned to Otto was the recaning of a set of 18th-century chairs. He took them away in his van and when he returned with them I was horrified at what I saw. They were poorly done, and they had not finished off properly or tidily at all. When I made some comment to him to this effect he said: 'Oh, I gave those to a fellow I met in the pub who does a bit of caning.'

Otto, I noticed, spent much of his time in the Apple Chamber and one afternoon he came across two carved wooden dolphins each about 5ft long. He drew these to the attention of Lady Scarsdale and persuaded her to let him gild them and suggested they would provide a fine ornamental pelmet to grace the curtains in the sitting room. I had some misgivings over this, but Lady Scarsdale seemed all for the project.

Gilding requires considerable skill in handling gold leaf and gold size; skill which Otto did not have. When he had finished with the dolphins, instead of being a beautiful mellow tone, burnished by the use of agate stone, they came back dazzlingly bright, brassy and vulgar looking. Two beautiful carvings had been ruined in my opinion. All the details of the carving were now lost, the incisions and nooks and crannies all crudely bunged up with gold leaf of dubious quality.

'Come and help me get these up,' he said. 'A surprise for Tilla.'

With serious misgivings this time I fetched a stepladder and between us we managed to hoist the dolphins into position.

As soon as Lady Scarsdale saw them she reeled back in horror. Aghast, she said to me: 'Get them down, Adams. Get them down at once. Quickly. Before his lordship sees them.'

Down they came and were stored away. What became of them after that I do not know. I never saw them again.

While rummaging through the Apple Chamber, Otto had also come across the glazed doors to the set of bookcases in the Library. I imagine that with poor atmospheric conditions in the room they had been removed years before, possibly by Lord Curzon, to allow air to circulate more freely around the early leather-bound volumes. Otto now decided a lucrative job for him would be to repair and rehang all these doors. Each one had glazing bars arranged in patterns but I imagine some of these needed replacing as well as some of the small panes of glass. Again the whole restoration was done in cheapskate fashion. Where there had been three hinges before, Otto now replaced these with two, and the glazing bars which before had been held in place with putty were now pinned into position. What particularly annoyed Tommy Brown was that when he came into the house at the end of winter for his annual task of polishing the floors, the floorboards in the Library were littered with hundreds of pins which Otto had failed to clear away. They not only scratched the floor but also worked their way into Tommy's electric polisher. For months afterwards he was still finding pins everywhere.

On one occasion when Lord and Lady Scarsdale were away for a short holiday I noticed two vans parked outside the door to the Apple Chamber and Otto together with an assistant of his was busily loading a number of pieces of furniture into the back. I felt some anxiety about this manoeuvre and decided to challenge him.

'What are you doing removing so much stuff? Does Lady Scarsdale know about it?'

He looked startled for a moment but soon regained composure.

'Of course she does. She said I could take my choice of articles from the Apple Chamber as payment for the restoration work I've done.'

I was dubious about this but I could hardly stop Otto going off with his haul. I decided to mention the matter to Lady Scarsdale when she returned. A few days later, when I was in our sitting room enjoying a two-hour break, I heard an almighty crash and the splintering of glass in the courtyard below. Hurrying to the window, I saw furniture coming hurtling through one of the windows of the Apple Chamber. I hurried through the adjoining door and discovered Lady Scarsdale having one of her 'fits', throwing chairs and stools and anything she could handle through the window. The first chair she had thrown had obviously broken the already shaky window frame and provided her with an easy route for other stuff.

CHAPTER 18

It was not surprising, considering the length of time I was at Kedleston, that there were certain occasions when my patience was stretched to the limit and beyond. Such an occurrence followed Lord and Lady Scarsdale's return from a short visit to London.

The day had started badly. Early on, one of the cleaning women had reported to me that the television in the sitting room was not working. I wondered how she knew this, since although it came within the scope of her duties to dust the television set, she had no business to be switching it on. I assumed that perhaps the women amused themselves watching television when they knew the Scarsdales were away.

Whatever the rights and wrongs of that, my concern now was to get the set in working order by the time the Scarsdales returned. There were certain programmes, *The Saint* was one of them, which they never missed and would have been extremely put out to have done so. When their favourite programmes were on, instead of serving dinner in the dining room I took supper trays up to them in the sitting room.

I now examined the television set myself, realised I could not put it right and phoned a TV repair company. They sent a man immediately.

The technician was able to remedy the fault and he was just driving away from the north forecourt when Lord and Lady Scarsdale arrived.

'Who was that, Adams?' her ladyship asked, catching sight of the departing vehicle.

'Just the television man, m'Lady.'

'What's he doing here?'

'Well, I thought it best to make sure the television was working properly for you on your return.'

I congratulated myself on having acquired over the years some diplomatic skills in the presentation of information to them.

I carried Lord and Lady Scarsdale's luggage up to their rooms and before leaving Lady Scarsdale with her maid I reminded her that I would need the jewellery that she had taken with her so that I could return it to the strong room. On this occasion, for a function of some importance, she had chosen to take with her the 18th-century diamonds, a pair of coral and pearl earrings and a Victorian gold and aquamarine brooch. While the Scarsdales were away I slept with the remainder of the jewellery in a bag under my pillow at night, which I considered safer than leaving it in the strong room. There were no burglar alarms at that time at Kedleston.

Lady Scarsdale now handed the jewellery bag over to me and I took it down to the butler's pantry where I was in the midst of cleaning the silver. I checked the contents and found everything there except the coral and pearl earrings. I assumed her ladyship's maid, Mrs Payne, was still unpacking and that she would find them and bring them down to me.

No one came downstairs so eventually I went to Lady Scarsdale with the bag in hand and had a word with her.

'I'm afraid I haven't got the coral earrings here, m'Lady.'

'Yes, you have. They're in the bag with the other things.'

'No, m'Lady, I'm afraid they're not. They must still be in one of your cases.'

She seemed a little annoyed at being contradicted but said she would have a look and send them down to me when they were found.

Downstairs in the pantry I continued cleaning the silver. The maid did not come with the earrings, so after a while I went upstairs again to remind Lady Scarsdale. She called Mrs Payne and the two of them assured me there was nothing in the suitcases.

'You must have them, Adams. I had them in London and I put them away after wearing them. Of course I did. Mrs Payne hasn't seen them, so they must be in there with the other things.'

'But I'm afraid they're not, m'Lady. Would you let me go through your cases? They may have slipped down the side somewhere.'

'No. There's no need for that.' She was getting a bit short with me now. 'Mrs Payne has checked all the cases and I am satisfied. There's absolutely no need for you to go through them.'

'But she may have missed something. Two pairs of eyes are better than one. Please let me have a look.'

'No. Once and for all, Adams, I've told you they're not there.'

'Well, I'll have to make a note that they're missing. They're on the inventory you know.'

Lady Scarsdale seemed rather taken aback and a little scared at my mention of the inventory.

I returned to my cleaning in the butler's pantry. A few minutes later Lord Scarsdale came down.

'These earrings, Adams. Are you sure you haven't got them?'

'Quite sure, m'Lord. I'm more then sure. I'm positive I haven't got them.'

'Are you quite sure you haven't let them drop on the floor or into the rubbish bin here? You probably put them on the table with the silver and they fell off into the basket below.'

I pulled out the basket he had mentioned and emptied the contents on to the floor. Out fell some old cleaning cloths, yesterday's newspaper and wrappers from my glucose tablets but, as I already knew, no earrings.

'Well it's your responsibility, Adams. You must know where they are. Her ladyship brought them back to this house.'

With that he strode off, all but accusing me of having them. He did not go as far as saying: 'You've got them. Where are they?' But his manner and tone implied it. I went upstairs again to have a word with Mrs Payne.

'Look, don't tell her ladyship but get the cases out, put them in the Adam room and let me go through them.'

'But they're not there. I've been through all the bags and cases several times so there's no point in you looking.'

By now I was getting more than short-tempered. 'Just do it, woman. Take the cases there and let me look.'

Still she refused and while we continued arguing I could hear Lady Scarsdale on the phone. She returned to say 'I've rung the hotel in London, Adams. His lordship thinks you've taken them but I suppose it's just possible I didn't pack them. I've rung the hotel and told them to start a search of all the staff and all the rooms.'

The manager rang back about half an hour later to say nothing had been found. He had every confidence in the staff, he said, but they would look further into the matter. By this time Lady Scarsdale had worked herself into quite a panic. She remembered a suspicious-looking foreigner she had seen at the hotel. The police were alerted and she phoned her son Mr Richard, who was a diamond merchant in Hatton Garden. He was too busy to speak to her but he phoned back a little later. By this time Lady Scarsdale was in no state to take any calls so I answered the phone and spoke to Mr Richard. He was the only one showing any sense.

'Look, Adams, it's no use my talking to mother while she's in this state. Will you please tell her to stop all this nonsense at once. It seems Interpol have been alerted now because of the foreigner she mentioned and all kinds of problems will be set in motion. It'll be in the papers in no time at all and who knows where it will end. The wretched earrings just aren't worth bothering about. If they don't turn up I'll get some replacements for her to the same value.'

Meanwhile, Lord Scarsdale had come up with another theory. 'You don't think the television man stole them, do you, Adams?'

'Good grief, m'Lord, of course he didn't take them. He'd gone before you even set foot in the house.'

But Lady Scarsdale when she heard this convinced herself that he was the culprit. I had to put her right on that point.

'M'Lady, the television man has not stolen your earrings. There is no possible way he could have taken them. He'd packed up his tools and you saw him getting into his van, and asked who he was, as he was driving away. Now let's have no more of this nonsense. No one has stolen your earrings. They have been mislaid somehow.'

'But if they have been stolen – '

'They have not been stolen. There's no one in this house wants to steal your jewellery. You took them away and I haven't had them back. That's all there is to it. If they don't turn up Mr Richard will find you a replacement. The bank comes only once a year to check the inventory and that's not due for some time yet, so there's nothing to worry about.'

But Lady Scarsdale was now weeping uncontrollably. 'No, they've been stolen. I know they've been stolen.'

At this point Mrs Payne went up to her and put her arms around her and said 'Oh, m'Lady, m'Lady. There now.'

This was too much for me. My patience was finally exhausted. I rounded on the two of them and said 'Yes, Mrs Payne, you take m'Lady out of this bloody room and m'Lady her somewhere else. Get out of my sight the pair of you. Go and cry on each other's shoulders somewhere else. Good god, you'd think the crown jewels had been stolen.'

Having had my say I went downstairs, aware that my diplomatic skills had plummeted. I was angry and upset that after all this time it appeared they had no trust in me at all. Everything I did in the house was for their benefit – to keep them happy, to make life easy for them, to try and avoid situations like the one we were now plunged into. There would be unpleasantness in the house for days. I tried to calm my agitation with some vigorous cleaning of the silver.

A few minutes later there was an almighty scream which reverberated from the top of the house right down to the butler's pantry. I went racing upstairs dreading what I was going to find.

Lady Scarsdale was running downstairs and we met on the first floor landing. For a moment I thought she was going to throw her arms around me.

'Oh, Adams, Adams,' she exclaimed. 'We've found them! Look, we've found them! Get me a bottle of champagne, quickly.'

I did not share her delight. I was still angry and upset at being virtually accused of stealing the earrings. I asked her where they had been found.

'Oh, Mrs Payne found them in the bottom of one of the zip-covers I keep my dresses in.'

'Well, I feel I must say m'Lady, that you should try and trust people a little more, then you wouldn't have to suffer in this way and get so upset.' Diplomacy had returned.

I fetched a bottle of Bollinger and served her ladyship. She was the only one who would be celebrating.

Later that day Lady Scarsdale asked me to bring her car round to the front door. She wanted to go into Derby. As she got into the car she said to me in the winsome tone she could assume when it suited her: 'Adams, let's forget all about this incident.'

'I've forgotten it already, m'Lady,' I replied.

I knew this was the nearest she would ever come to an apology.

CHAPTER 19

It was all set to be a routine day at Kedleston, one of those 'What shall do today, darling?' days; an attitude which I had come to detest. I had taken Lady Scarsdale's mail to her bedroom and then went on to his lordship to attend to his needs. These duties completed, I was returning along the corridor when the peace and quiet of the early morning was shattered.

'Adams! Adams! Quickly! Come here!'

I tapped on her ladyship's dressing room door and walked in. She was waving a letter about with great excitement, her face lit up with smiles. 'Prince Charles wants to come to dinner. Isn't that marvellous, Adams? What an honour.'

I did not receive the news with as much enthusiasm as she. Lady Scarsdale went on: 'No one is to know of this, Adams. I want absolute secrecy. I will tell cook later, of course.' She dropped a curtsy there and then, wobbled a bit, and said 'I'll have to do better than that, won't I?'

'I don't know, m'Lady,' I replied. 'What I do know is that my evening tail suit is hardly fit for a prince to see.' I reminded her that it had been one of Lord Scarsdale's old suits cut down to fit me. She immediately agreed to pay for a new suit for the auspicious occasion.

After she had recovered from her initial excitement, Lady Scarsdale's biggest problem was the choice of guests. And the most difficult choice of all was finding a partner for Charles. In her way she was known as a matchmaker and now she had the match of her life to arrange. She decided eventually on one of the Okeover girls, a daughter of Sir Ian Walker-Okeover, Lord Lieutenant of the county and a regular guest at Kedleston. It was to be a small dinner party of eight people: Lord and Lady Scarsdale, His Royal Highness and Miss Walker-Okeover, the Honourable Mr and Mrs Francis Curzon, and two others.

On the afternoon of the visit the hairdresser was summoned to Kedleston and Lady Scarsdale's long and luxuriant hair was washed and set on top of her head while her maid fussed and pampered her in other ways.

For the table Lady Scarsdale decided to use the four gold candlesticks designed by Robert Adam and made by Matthew Boulton. The centrepiece was to be a gold racing cup, a trophy decorated with nymphs and with a tall fluted lid, which was not in my opinion the most suitable centrepiece. It was absurdly tall and on a circular table for eight it obscured the view of each guest's opposite number. I thought she might have chosen the Georgian silver epergne surmounted by Jason and the Golden Fleece. But on reflection I realised that this also was too big.

I put out the rarely used linen covers trimmed with old Brussels lace, together with napkins. There were fine crystal and coloured glasses for wine and water, heavy George III silver salts with crossover dolphin feet, a Queen Anne freedom box, the Pierre Harache hot water jug and the silver and gold cock pheasants. There were also small silver dishes for each guest which they might use as ash trays or for nut shells or fruit skin. His Royal Highness was given Lady Scardale's favourite (also my own) beautiful plain silver Charles I wine taster.

The flatware settings for the four course meal were: early Georgian pudding spoons for the soup; Lord Curzon's fish eaters; George III three-pronged meat forks and silver-hafted knives with steel blades; George III silver-gilt dessert spoons and forks; and small three-pronged forks with matching silver knives for the savoury.

Lady Scarsdale got out her own early Worcester and Derby plates, all top quality beautiful pieces, and her rare Derby coffee cans of the Duesbury period.

I must say the table looked magnificent when set but then it looked magnificent for every dinner party, and such a show of wealth was probably nothing out of the ordinary for Prince Charles.

This being a very rare occasion, Lord Scarsdale came with me down to the cellar to choose the wine. Only on one other occasion had he come with me to the cellar, the time when, as I liked to put it, I took port with a peer of the realm. On that occasion he picked out a bottle of old Caleb, encrusted with the dirt of ages, and said 'I'll show you how to decant a bottle of port, Adams.' It must have escaped his notice that I had been decanting port for them for many years.

'Light a candle.'

I lit a candle and set it upon a thrall at eye level. I broke the wax seal on the bottle and withdrew the cork. He picked up an old pewter funnel which was lying there, put it in the decanter and, holding it in front of the candle, he started to decant the contents of the bottle. After a few gurgles he stopped and began to tell me a tale about his first wife, Mildred, and how she suffered from tuberculosis. He sent her to Switzerland to try various cures. One of the physicians told him to give her plenty of port. At this stage he had just about filled the decanter and was down to the lees in the bottle. Looking round, he said: 'There's a glass here somewhere, Adams.'

I knew there was a broken Georgian glass, sheared diagonally across from top to bottom so that it held about an egg-cupful. It was filthy and must have been lying there for many years before I ever went to Kedleston.

'That's it. That's fine,' he said.

He took the glass, poured the lees into it and handed it to me. 'There you are. Drink that up. It'll do you good.'

I thanked him and put it on the thrall. He carried on looking for the wines he wanted for luncheon that day. After a few minutes he turned, picked up the broken glass and downed the sludge himself. It was the only time I ever saw him take a drink, if you could call it that.

This time while we were there he spotted two dust-covered bottles of Edward VII Burton Ale, which he suggested I might offer to Prince Charles' man.

The Prince arrived about seven o'clock, driving himself in a Land Rover and accompanied by just one detective/bodyguard. Lord Scarsdale stood at the front door of the family wing while Lady Scarsdale walked out on to the forecourt to greet His Royal Highness. The weeks of curtsy practising had achieved the desired result. With the grace of a ballerina she executed a faultless low curtsy, the soft folds of her ball gown floating in a large circle around her as she did so. I could not help thinking how beautiful a woman she was, although then in her 70s or thereabouts.

With the introductions completed, Prince Charles was given a tour of the state rooms. While the tour was in progress the other guests arrived and I showed them up to the sitting room ready to be introduced. Promptly at eight o'clock I announced: 'Dinner is served' and Lady Scarsdale led His Royal Highness downstairs and to his place at the table. As I recall, the conversation was mainly about the Prince's charity work. I also remember thinking it odd that Lord Scarsdale addressed him as Sire, rather than Sir, throughout the visit.

The cook at the time was Mrs Fleetwood, the successor to Cookie Wilson. Mrs Fleetwood was not a particularly good cook. By now we were, if not exactly scraping, certainly nearing the bottom of the barrel as far as cooks went. Mrs Fleetwood's credentials were no more than having run a greasy spoon café in an alley off the High Street in Burton upon Trent, followed by a stint with a coffee stall on the recreation ground and a short period with a Derbyshire family, the Chandos Poles. She was a nervous woman and had two great faults. One was that she used an electric mixer. This would not have been a fault in itself had she known how to use the machine properly. I believe that when you use such an appliance the mixing is done in seconds. Most light things need no longer than this. But not so with Mrs Fleetwood. She would put the mixture in the container, turn the machine to its highest setting and then walk away. She would start cleaning windows or phone an order through to the grocer in Derby. Consequently the ingredients were over mixed with all the air beaten out of them, and her meringues and soufflés were usually a failure. Her other fault was that she was rather absent minded. Sometimes she would put things in the freezer and then completely forget about them. Possibly she had a lot on her mind. I was later to learn that she and her husband were deep in debt.

I recalled an occasion during Mrs Fleetwood's time when the Duke and Duchess of Devonshire were visiting Kedleston and there had occurred a mishap, or, as Lady Scarsdale saw it, a disaster, during luncheon. There were eight at table and the menu was consommé, followed by saddle of lamb and then strawberry mousse. Lady Scarsdale always liked her white wine not merely chilled but semi-frozen – that is chilled to the point where it was just pourable. Bearing this in mind, I put into the fridge about 12 o'clock six bottles of white wine (the rule being one bottle of wine per two guests with two others in reserve). At the time I warned Mrs Fleetwood that there were more bottles than usual in the fridge. She, I noticed, was busy churning the mousse in her infernal machine.

I served the first two courses without mishap. The saddle of lamb was cleared away and I set out the pudding plates and poured the white wine while we were waiting for the next course to arrive from the kitchen. The strawberry mousse eventually came through the hatch in a glass bowl which I realised, as I lifted it to place on a silver serving tray, was icy cold and already frosting over. I wrapped a napkin round as I usually did with chilled wine bottles.

The Duchess, as guest of honour, was sitting on Lord Scarsdale's right. Picking up the silver tray, I went to her left to offer her the dish first as etiquette demanded. She was engaged in conversation as she picked up the silver serving spoon to take a portion. The spoon failed to make any impression on the surface of the mousse and the Duchess waved it and me away with a gesture of dismissal.

I next offered the mousse to Lord Scarsdale. He prodded it with the spoon which this time shot out of his hand and across the room, startling everyone into silence for a few moments. I fetched another spoon, and, holding the tray on the palm of my left hand and steadying the glass dish with my right, I again offered it to Lord Scarsdale. This time he took both spoon and fork to it. The silver fork penetrated a little way and then bent like a piece of cutlery in the hands of Uri Geller. I was now in a quandary, realising the mousse was frozen solid and wondering what I was going to serve in its place if I took the dish away. I always had spare plates and cutlery ready on my serving table for cases of emergency but it was beyond me or the cook to produce another pudding at short notice; however, Lady Scarsdale now intervened, saying 'I think you'd better take that away, Adams. We've had a bit of a disaster, haven't we?'

'I'm afraid we have, m'Lady.'

I took the frozen mousse away and removed the unused plates and cutlery from each guest and we went on to the biscuits and cheese.

Later that afternoon when the guests had departed Lady Scarsdale said to me 'What happened, Adams?'

I told her I believed Mrs Fleetwood had over mixed the mousse in her machine and it had gone runny. She had then put it in the freezer hoping it would set a bit and forgotten about it. Mrs Fleetwood's version, not surprisingly, was different. She blamed me for filling the fridge with extra bottles of wine leaving her no space for the mousse other than in the freezer.

Nothing more was said but I knew the luncheon had been a failure in Lady Scarsdale's eyes. The talk in high circles would be that she had been entertaining the first lady of the county who had a superb French chef at Chatsworth while she, her hostess, had a woman who could not even make a mousse.

Now, for Prince Charles' visit, Lady Scarsdale had wisely persuaded Mrs Fleetwood to attempt nothing more ambitious than a cold consommé, poached fish, a meat course and a savoury of cheese straws. All went well until the cheese straws came through the hatch. I was expecting them to be thin as matchsticks, delicate in appearance. Instead they came to me looking more like bundles of swollen fingers and I felt embarrassed at having to offer them to His Royal Highness. They were to be eaten from beautiful, small silver plates. They seemed to me to be an insult to both Prince Charles and the plates.

The detective ate his meal in my butler's pantry but I had little time to talk to him. He consumed the two bottles of beer with apparent relish despite their age. I gave him a guidebook and let him into the state rooms and suggested that later he wander in the grounds.

Prince Charles left about 10 o'clock to drive to Chatsworth, where he was staying. Nothing, of course, came of the matchmaking with Miss Walker-Okeover. Some time later Lady Scarsdale came to me with a little present.

'Here you are, Adams. This is for you, for helping out with Prince Charles' visit.'

It was a small filigree photograph frame.

CHAPTER 20

During these years my work as butler left me very little time to think about what direction my life was taking, but I did become increasingly aware that I was sacrificing any sort of family life I might have enjoyed and even neglecting my family responsibilities for what seemed to be my all consuming job. I still worked on average about 14 hours a day.

After 10 years or so Betty and I were aware that some assessment of the situation was needed. We had long since realised that we would never be able to save enough for the house we had originally hoped to buy. What concerned me now was not so much getting away from the place as having some security. As the years went by and I observed Lord Scarsdale showing signs of his age it set me thinking about what might happen to me when Francis Curzon succeeded to the title. I knew very little about Curzon but Newton had told me many years before that when he inherited and came to live at the Hall he would bring his own butler and his own staff with him.

I decided to approach Lady Scarsdale with my worries. She was the more approachable of the two. It was no use going to his lordship.

I asked Lady Scarsdale if she could give me some idea of what might happen to me when his lordship passed on and she herself would have to leave the Hall.

'I'm anxious,' I told her, 'about my security, as you must understand. After all I've done for this house I find myself with nothing behind me. We can only just live on the wages so I have very little money put by in the bank and no pension to look forward to. I've no house of my own and I could easily find myself without a job or accommodation.'

'There's no need for you to worry about that, Adams,' she replied. 'You're quite secure. I'm sure Mr Curzon will look after you. But if you're really concerned we could perhaps get a little agreement drawn up for you. Something to set your mind at rest.'

At about the same time Tommy Brown, who knew of my predicament, mentioned that there was a cottage in Weston Underwood, the village where he lived, which had apparently been taken over by squatters. It was in a very private and secluded position up a narrow lane called Thimble Hill.

The cottage, Thisker, was let to a tenant farmer as part of his agreement and was intended to serve as accommodation for one of his farm hands. How squatters had got there I do not know. Tommy Brown had a theory that the farmer had at first been subletting and paying the agent a back-hander to turn a blind eye. Whatever the case, Lord and Lady Scarsdale knew nothing of what was going on. The squatters, whom Tommy believed to be students, were making rather a nuisance of themselves in the quiet little village, and I saw it would obviously suit him to have them dislodged and Betty and me living there.

Tommy suggested we go and look at the place one afternoon when the students were away. When we arrived we found we had to climb in as the door was some 3 or 4ft above ground level. There must have been a flight of steps up to it at one time but these were no longer there.

After my experience of the cottage in Kedleston village I was not entirely surprised at the scene of filth and dereliction which met my eye. I made a few notes of what essential work I considered needed doing before anyone could move in.

Afternoon tea, as I have mentioned, was Lord Scarsdale's favourite meal. I decided to broach the subject one afternoon when he was enjoying his sandwiches and cake and I might hope to catch him in a good mood. I took the tea tray up to the sitting room and placed it in front of him. Before I could say anything, Lord Scarsdale, who must have got word of what was afoot, raised the matter himself.

'This cottage in Weston Underwood, Adams. I'd be delighted for you to have it. What I shall do is give you a note to take to the paint suppliers and if you're prepared to paint the place in your own time you can move in as soon as you like.'

'Thank you. That's very kind of you, m'Lord,' I said. 'But there are just one or two things I feel I ought to draw your attention to first. There are a few problems you're probably not aware of.'

I took the list from my pocket and began to read it out. 'It requires, m'Lord, a new roof, a dozen new windows, new ceilings upstairs, two fireplaces downstairs, a front door and a back door, new bath, new kitchen sink, steps to the front door – '

At this point Lord Scarsdale got up, pushed past me and strode out leaving his tea untouched. Lady Scarsdale and I exchanged looks of mutual sympathy. It was seven o'clock before his lordship returned to the house.

A few days later he appeared to have calmed down. He said to me: 'Can you spare a minute, Adams? I want you to come with me and look at this cottage we've been talking about.'

So we took the Land Rover and drove the two miles or so to Weston Underwood. Thimble Hill was so overgrown the Land Rover could scarcely get up the lane.

I, of course, had some idea of what we were going to see but Lord Scarsdale was speechless. He ran his eye over the appalling state of the place. A poster of Che Guevara stared down at him and Chinese writing was daubed in red paint on every wall. There were no beds in the cottage but two single wardrobes with their doors removed were lying on the floor and acted as makeshift beds. One, we noticed, was filled with hundreds of photographs of naked women. There was evidence that a dog had been chained to the wall, old oil cans were scattered about and part of a car engine had been shoved into the fireplace in the downstairs front room.

Still speechless, Lord Scarsdale turned and walked out. He strode through Tommy Brown's garden, trampling flower beds as he went, jumped down into the lane and ran down into the hollow where the farmhouse stood. He burst inside shouting as he entered.

'Eyre! Where are you?' Eyre was not there and it was his wife who took the brunt of his lordship's anger. 'Tell him to report to the estate office a soon as he gets back. I'm taking the cottage off him, and I want to see him in the estate office today.'

A few weeks later Tommy Brown told me that work had started on the cottage. He and his sister, who also lived in Weston Underwood, kept me informed of the work in progress. Their reports were not encouraging. The firm set on to do the renovation immediately subcontracted the work to third-rate jobbing bricklayers, plasterers and joiners who took little pride in anything they did. Most of the things on my list were carried out after a fashion but the most important one – the new roof – was not done, with disastrous consequences later.

When the cottage was finally habitable, Lady Scarsdale told me they were arranging for their solicitor to draw up a 20-year lease for me. When we moved in she also very kindly bought me a moped to use to get to work each day. I think she was scared of losing me then. It was difficult to get butlers in those days of the mid-70s.

Betty and I were thrilled when the lease eventually came through. The Scarsdales' solicitor told us that we were now safe for life, and on the strength of this Betty and I sunk what little savings we had into further improvements to the cottage and garden.

Meanwhile, my work at the Hall continued as before. That summer Lord Scarsdale informed me that he was negotiating the sale of one of his machine guns and asked me if I would take it to Birmingham for him. He suggested that Mrs Adams might like to go with me, and since Betty and I did not get out very often I thought it would make a welcome change in routine. Lord Scarsdale gave me the address of the dealer and told me to take the Land Rover for the day. We put the machine gun under a piece of sacking in the back of the vehicle and set off.

We drove down the A38 towards Lichfield, feeling elated at our escape for the day. We turned south and eventually negotiated the newly opened Spaghetti Junction. But then we got completely lost in the back streets of the city and seemed to be driving around endlessly. Eventually, seeing a policeman on duty, I stopped to ask directions.

It was not until later that I realised how naïve I had been. At that time the IRA were already active in Birmingham and there was I, with the good Irish Catholic name of Adams, driving along with an Irishwoman sitting beside me in the front seat and a machine gun hidden in the back of the Land Rover. It was fortunate that Betty, with her still strong Irish brogue, had not extended a friendly greeting to the policeman.

With IRA troubles on the increase and more stringent regulations concerning firearms coming into force, Lord Scarsdale was not so fortunate. Soon after my visit to Birmingham the police had reason to come to Kedleston. There had been trouble on the estate with poachers. A police sergeant arrived at the Hall and I escorted him through the Armoury Corridor on the way to the family wing. In the corridor he spotted the remaining machine gun and asked me one or two questions about it. He then conducted his business with Lord Scarsdale and left.

The next day he returned with a senior officer. The upshot was that they wanted to examine all the guns Lord Scarsdale had, and they confiscated the majority of them. The only ones they let him keep were the shooting guns, including his Purdeys. He had not mentioned the revolvers, of course, so they remained hidden in his bedroom. He tried to explain to the police that all his guns were harmless, that they had not been fired since World War One and in any case the firing mechanisms were de-activated. The Inspector pointed out that they could soon be made usable again by any competent gunsmith. They gave him a receipt and took the guns away to Nottingham, telling him he would get them back when the emergency was over.

The first winter we spent in Thisker, rain and snow began coming in through the roof. The estate got hold of a local handyman to do some emergency repairs. He cut all the overhangs from the roof, which was virtually the death knell of the cottage. The parts of the walls which had never been exposed to the weather were so dry and porous that they soaked up every drop of moisture, and within a few months the bedroom walls were black with mould.

I told Lady Scarsdale that it was impossible for us to continue at Thisker and that I'd like to move somewhere else if possible. Very soon another cottage, Brook Willows in Kedleston village, became available. The lease on Thisker was transferred to Brook Willows and on Christmas Eve Betty and I moved into our fourth home on the estate.

CHAPTER
21

It was during the early months of my 13th year as butler (my 15th at Kedleston) that the stress and strain of the work began to manifest itself in a serious way.

For those 13 years I had worked on average 14 hours a day, for periods of 24–28 days in succession, after which I was entitled to a four-day break. But I found that I rarely had four days to myself. It had become the custom that on the first day of what should have been my holiday I would prepare breakfast for Lord and Lady Scarsdale (cook was off for the same four days and she always left the evening before), press his lordship's clothes, polish his shoes, pack his case, clear away the breakfast things and then run them to the station so that they could catch the train to London. On my return from the station I had to put away in the strong room all the silver that was in everyday use. These duties meant that I lost half a day of my holiday straight away. It was also taken for granted that on the fourth day I would collect them from the station on their return, unpack their cases, bring out the silver, prepare and serve supper, and wash up afterwards.

The physical symptoms of my decline were several. The most obvious one was that after 13 years of continually running along stone corridors and up and down stone staircases I had trouble with my feet. I had read somewhere that Margot Fonteyn recommended Epsom salts for treating ballet dancers' feet, so I bought a bag of coarse Epsom salts from the chemist, made up a solution with hot water and soaked my feet as often as I could. Another aspect was that the bones in my ankles began to crack in an alarming manner as I hurried about my duties, sounding like machine-gun fire. I also suffered from severe backache and general exhaustion. Whenever I had a spare moment I would lie on my back on the floor with my feet raised over a chair, the only relief I could find.

I remembered how in my days as houseman Newton had exhibited these same signs of fatigue. But Newton had worked six years, found it necessary to leave for a while, and then returned after a period of recovery to continue for another six years. I had served 12 years as butler without a break.

One of the causes of my exhaustion was the way in which the house was organised. Newton had been promised an under-butler to assist him but nothing had come of it. I had briefly been given a footman in the shape of John Hurst with his bunions and back trouble, who left after a month. Whenever male guests were staying I had to act as valet for them as well as Lord Scarsdale, which meant extra suits to press and shoes to clean, and this added considerably to the burden of work. Some of the rules which Lady Scarsdale invented also made the work more arduous, the worst one being that the butler and no one else should wash up every single item of porcelain, silver and glass used at their table.

Betty, feeling a resentment even keener than mine, was driven on one occasion to speak out. It was late one evening after a dinner party at which Betty had been helping. We were in the kitchen finishing the washing up together when Lady Scarsdale came in and upbraided me over some minor matter.

This was too much for Betty, who turned on Lady Scarsdale. 'You should be grateful for having such a man to wait on you,' she said to her. 'He's worked himself into the ground for you and you hardly seem to notice it. You don't realise it's too much for him to run this place virtually single-handed. You've got a good man and you've got him for nothing. You've got both of us for nothing.'

Lady Scarsdale looked at Betty in astonishment, then turned to me. 'Get her home at once Adams,' she said. 'Call the doctor. You're wife's obviously not well.'

Over the years the pattern of the Scarsdales' lives had changed. They took fewer holidays – eventually no holidays at all – and instead did more entertaining at Kedleston which, of course, meant more work for me. They held frequent luncheon parties which extended my working time into the afternoons and cut into the two-hour break I was supposed to have.

The mental strains too had grown over the years. Like Newton before me I began to resent more and more the lives which Lord and

Lady Scarsdale led. The 'What shall we do today, darling?' syndrome made me very angry. If they had done something useful with their lives I don't think I would have minded wearing myself out for them. But they contributed little for the privileges they enjoyed. Lord Scarsdale attended the House of Lords only when summoned. One of the few occasions he addressed the Upper House was when he opposed Lady Summerskill's bill to abolish boxing. Lady Scarsdale was required to attend a meeting of the NSPCC once a year and make a little speech since her name appeared on the headed paper as patron – and it was the greatest burden in the world to her. She had to be rewarded merely for doing a bit of gardening. 'Adams, fetch me a bottle of champagne. I've just dead-headed 200 roses.' Yes, I thought, and left 200 flower heads for other people to clear away.

On another occasion she came hurrying up from one of the lakes. 'Oh Adams, help me get these boots off. I've just rescued Tarquin. He was entangled in the reeds. He would have drowned. I've been up to my neck in the water. Just look at me.'

Up to her neck? I couldn't help noticing that her clothing was completely dry – even her boots. But I said nothing. A few weeks later a medal arrived from the RSPCA. Lady Scarsdale showed it to me and said: 'Put this up in the trophy corridor, Adams, where people can see it.'

I think what kept me going for so long was the memory of Newton's words: 'They only want you while you're on your feet.' I knew that if I took time off sick I would be in danger of losing my position. The terms of employment in private service bore no resemblance to regulations elsewhere. There were, as far as I knew, no rights for employees, no obligations on the part of the employer to grant sick leave, or statutory holidays. Betty had for a long time been wanting me to give up the job, saying that we would get by somehow and that now we had the security of a lease we would not be homeless. But realising how difficult it would be for me to get other work (I was then in my mid-50s), I asked Lady Scarsdale if I might have one day off every week instead of going 28 days without a break and then getting at most only two completely free days. After due consideration they grudgingly granted my request. This was a help, if only to remind my employers that I too was human.

It was an arrangement which may have suited them better too. By this time Lord Scarsdale was far from well. He was suffering from senile dementia and finding it difficult to travel to London and spend four days at his club every so often.

The day they told me to take off was Monday. On Sunday evenings I set out in the pantry all the silver that would be needed the following day – breakfast silver, lunch silver and dinner silver – so that it was all ready for whoever would be looking after them. Lady Scarsdale did not relax her rule about washing up, so the first thing I had to do on Tuesday before starting my usual workload was all Monday's washing up. Slowly over the ensuing weeks my strength declined still further, until one night on my return from work Betty said I must give in my notice – no matter what. And I too realised there must now be and end to this.

The next morning I went to talk to the Commodore. The Commodore had by now retired and was living in Cross Stitch flat at the top of the main body of the house. It had not been his original intention to spend his remaining days at Kedleston. During his long shore leaves he had often told me how friends in the West Indies very much wanted him to settle with them but that he was planning to buy a villa in the Algarve and hoping to retire there with his First Officer.

For about 10 years or so the Commodore had gradually been bringing his possessions to Kedleston, where they were stored in the old schoolroom on the ground floor. This had perhaps given Lady Scarsdale the idea that he would spend his retirement at the Hall. Her interest in the Commodore had in no way abated. When he was at sea she was fretful and morose, but once she knew his ship had left South America on the homeward run she was a different character. Whenever the time of his arrival approached she was impatient beyond measure.

Eventually the schoolroom was packed to the ceiling with wooden crates and boxes. I used to go in once a week to open the shutters and air the place. I had to edge my way among the crates and when I reached the windows I could barely open the shutters half way.

One day Tommy Brown came to me just before lunch in a very agitated state. He and an outside worker had been instructed to report to the old schoolroom to assist Lady Scarsdale. She told them that everything stored in the room had to be unpacked and taken up to Cross Stitch flat on the second floor. This was a daunting task for any two men to tackle. The small Victorian lift could carry only two people, which meant that with the exception of a few packages everything had to be manhandled up the steep twisting back-stairs. There were beds, wardrobes, tables and chairs, chests large and small, pictures, porcelain, linen, pots and pans – almost every conceivable article needed to furnish a small house.

It was not the struggling and the carrying upstairs that had upset Tommy (for he always did any job at his own pace – slowly); it was the manner in which Lady Scarsdale had set about the task. She had suddenly become a woman demented, had begun to tear open packages and crates with complete disregard for the contents and had even broken a number of pieces. I do not know what caused this sudden outburst but I have always imagined she must have somehow heard, perhaps through talk at a dinner party, of the Commodore's intention to settle in Portugal.

At the time of Lady Scarsdale's outburst the Commodore was on a return journey from the Amazon, and all the time I had a feeling that he knew nothing of what was going on or that his retirement was being organised for him. Apparently 'Operation Cross Stitch' was being carried out as a surprise. I did not feel it my place to ask any questions as I had not been involved in the removal of his belongings, but I began to feel apprehensive about his reaction when he realised what had happened.

On the day of his arrival Lady Scarsdale instructed me to keep him away from the schoolroom at all costs, and to take his luggage up to his bedroom as usual. If he brought any more crates with him these were to be left in the corridor. I was not a witness to his reaction to the 'surprise' nor did he ever pass any comment to me. The villa in Portugal was never mentioned again.

When he retired he received telegrams and letters from all over the world, many of them expressing surprise that he had settled at

Kedleston. The incident has always remained a mystery but I am convinced that it was Lady Scarsdale who persuaded him to spend his retirement with her at Kedleston, where they both remained until his lordship died.

Now in my present predicament, I wanted the Commodore to know what I was about to do and why. I was anxious that it would not appear that I was giving up soon after I had got a lease and security on a cottage for Betty and myself. The Commodore said he was aware of my situation and was sad that it had come about. He had noticed how ill I appeared and thought I might have TB. He said he would talk to Lord and Lady Scarsdale, though he felt they would not change much in what they expected and demanded of their staff. He did talk to them, but they felt unable to help me in any way.

So I resigned my post giving one month's notice. Lord Scarsdale made no comment; Lady Scarsdale asked for six weeks' notice, which I agreed to. This eventually extended to a period of six months, taking me into the shooting season and another Christmas to get through before they could find a man to replace me.

The Commodore knew what a state I was reduced to but he was cast in a different mould from the Scarsdales. They knew what I had to do in the house but were totally unaware of the strain involved. I believe Helene Curzon, the wife of Francis Curzon, Lord Scarsdale's heir, although she came infrequently to the house, had a slightly better inkling of what I was doing. She looked in on me one morning while I was laying the table for a formal tea in the Blue Room.

'Oh, Adams,' she said. 'You're always working.'

'Someone has to bend their back to be whipped,' I replied. By now I was beyond being tactful.

When I left, Lady Scarsdale said they were going to let me live rent free in the cottage for one year while I 'sorted myself out'. It had not occurred to me that I would receive any parting gift and I was grateful for this generous gesture on their part. Lady Scarsdale also gave me the reference she had promised me so many years before, the one that would take me into any house in the country. But even had it been the key to paradise itself, I knew it was too late now for it to open any doors for me.

I finished work late one Sunday evening and handed the keys over to my successor. As I cycled back to the village, I felt no emotion other than relief.

CHAPTER 22

When I left the Hall it was as if I had been released from prison. For 15 years I had been cut off from the outside world. I'd had no time to read a newspaper, no time for my family, no time to think about anything other than looking after my two employers. I was a stranger to everything beyond the confines of Kedleston. I could not even find my way about Derby apart from the route to the station.

I had not given much thought as to what I might do. The first priority was to try and recover my health. The one thing I was determined not to do was to enter on any sort of domestic service and least of all be a butler anywhere. When Lady Scarsdale's brother heard I was leaving he had said: 'What will you do now, Adams? Off to the States? English butlers are always in demand there. The world's your oyster, you know.' If I had been a younger man and single I might have followed his suggestion. I had learnt too late that butlering is not for a married man.

On the first Monday I rested. On Tuesday morning I thought I would go to the Labour Exchange, as it was called then, and sign on. I was not familiar with procedure and my first brush with authority was not a happy one. I joined a massed crowd of the unemployed, long queues of men waiting their turn to be interviewed by the few clerks on duty. When my turn came a bespectacled young woman looked at me aggressively from behind a glass screen.

'When did you say finished work?'

'Sunday night'.

'Why didn't you come along yesterday then? That's when you should have been here.'

'I'm sorry. I didn't know. I didn't realise I had to come. I thought it was a choice I made, whether I applied for the dole or went out to look for work myself.'

Miss Superspecs became even more aggressive. 'You should have been here yesterday morning if you finished work on Sunday. Why did you finish? Were you fired?'

'No, of course I wasn't fired. I handed in my resignation.'

I watched as a black mark went down against me.

'You mean you deliberately put yourself out of work.'

'Of course not. I left because I was unable to carry on any longer. I was worked to the point of exhaustion.'

I realised I couldn't expect her to come anywhere near to understanding what it was like to be employed in a private household such as Kedleston, a kingdom to itself beyond the rules and regulations of the normal world.

'I didn't know I'd committed a crime by being a day late,' I said. 'But I'm here now and I'm not expecting you to pay me for Monday.'

A sardonic smile crept across her face. 'There's no question of you being paid at all until the statutory number of weeks has elapsed. The thing is – how do I know you really want to work?'

Her remark sickened me. I was glad I had not been mixed up in this sort of world if that was how it was now. I did not realise at the time just how many scroungers and cheats there were.

I went every week to the Labour Exchange to ask for work and look at the notice boards. I got the papers, wrote off for jobs but I got very few replies.

I was out of work for 10 months, which gave me plenty of time to reflect on my years at the Hall. From the personal point of view there had been rewards; not everything had been burdensome. I had been privileged to talk to many different people I would never have otherwise met. I felt pride when I walked through the state rooms among the splendid furnishings, the paintings and the silver. From these I learnt far more than I could ever have learnt from books. I knew too that I had given satisfaction to my employers. Lady Scarsdale appreciated what I did. What she did not appreciate was the difficulty of the job, the tremendous effort required to keep everything running smoothly in a house that was difficult to maintain at the best of times.

One day on my return from Derby I noticed Jack Gowan and the other estate workers hanging about by the parkland perimeter and I stopped to have a word with them.

'Hello, Mr Adams,' Jack said. 'Feeling better now?'

'Yes thanks. Much better. As a matter of fact I'm looking for work.' And then jokingly I added: 'I don't suppose you want a mate, do you, to help you with a bit of clearing up round here?'

He looked at me, shocked. 'Are you serious?'

'I'm desperate for any work, Jack. I've been looking for 10 months. I'd be happy to join you and the others.'

'Well, if you really are serious, I'll have a word with that bugger up there then.'

He was referring to Francis Curzon, Lord Scarsdale's heir, now agent for the estate, who took on all outside workers. Jack had a word and a short time later Curzon telephoned me. He told me he had spoken to Lord Scarsdale and that if I was prepared to come as an estate worker he would add my name to the payroll.

That year the wheel had turned full circle and I was at the bottom once more. I bought myself two stout pairs of boots and on Monday morning 25 April 1977 I set off up the drive from Village Lodge to begin my first day as a labourer on the estate.

I can be precise about the date I started as a labourer as I am now able to consult my one surviving diary, which tells me that the first few days in my new job were spent cutting logs, stacking fencing, repairing and sharpening tools, taking logs, coal and coke up to the Hall, and burning old and unwanted pieces of furniture.

We had our base at an area known as the Woodyard, set in the parkland some distance from the house, beyond the Adam Bridge. There was a low, two-storey brick building which may have predated the present Hall. Upstairs were huge joiners' benches, extending from one end of the building to the other. Around about were various sheds and a saw-pit, and at one time the whole area must have been a hive of industry for it was here, I believe, that timbers were cut for the building of the Hall; everything from massive roof timbers to floorboards, doors and window frames. But by my time the greater part of the Woodyard was in disuse, as if the whole area had been abandoned.

I was working with Jack Gowan, John Guest and several others. There was much dissatisfaction among the men, some of which was justified. Working conditions were poor. There was no lighting of any description in the cabin in the Woodyard, no water, no place to hang or dry clothes and nowhere for us to eat if required to stay all day. The toilet was primitive and there was litter and rubbish everywhere. The men had made no effort at all to clear up the mess. They had no incentive to help themselves. They preferred to stand about grumbling and complaining rather than do anything. The prevailing atmosphere was one of petty quarrels, idleness, shirking and discontent.

The second week I was working at the Gothic temple, an 18th-century folly on Cumber Hills, the lane running between Kedleston and the village of Duffield. This was where the head gamekeeper lived and here were the incubating rooms and the rearing pens. The fencing and wiring round the rearing field needed repairs. We had been asked to fit more posts but there were none with points cut. Gowan and

Guest would not sharpen the axe and did not seem to consider getting back the one good power saw which had been borrowed and not returned.

In May when the weather improved I was called up to the Hall to begin a programme of painting. I began by stripping and painting all the doors in the stable yard. This was a long job as all the old paint had to be chipped or burnt off, after which I gave each door three coats of paint. When the weather was wet I carried out a few bits of furniture restoration in the house and some minor electrical and plumbing work. Very little was provided in the way of equipment but I had permission from the Commodore to use his tools when I needed them.

My diary went on: 'I find myself continually thinking about life at the Hall and wondering what it was all about, what it was all for.'

June and July were spent on another programme of painting in the stable yard. This area was a small estate in itself, badly neglected over the years. In August I stripped the oil from the front doors of the Hall ready for re-oiling. My diary records: 'All my work so far has been has been hard, dirty and very uncomfortable. The "heavy gang" do little. They have been arriving at 10, leaving before midday, returning at two and breaking for the day just after four.'

I asked for permission to use the old joiner's shop, one of the outbuildings in the stable yard, and was told I might take it over as a workshop. The place was in a disgusting condition having been used as a rubbish dump for years and latterly by a builder, who lived in the village at the Schoolhouse but who had never cleared the place. It took eight hours' hard work to clear out the muck. Then, before anything more could be done, I had to determine the source of a bad and long-standing leak in the roof. This I discovered to be due to a broken tile, which I replaced with a good one. I then had to wait for the place to dry out before it could be used as a workshop. Meanwhile the whole area had to be cleaned a second time. The carpenter's bench which stood along one wall was full of dry rot and woodworm so I removed it, broke it up and burnt it. Where the bench had stood was a large hole which needed to be concreted over. Lady Scarsdale suggested placing an old door over the hole. This remark sickened me so much that I decided to leave everything as it was and await further, if any, developments.

Then in October that year Lord Scarsdale died.

CHAPTER 23

On the morning of 19 October 1977 I had just begun work in the joiner's shop when Francis Curzon came to me and said: 'Leave what you're doing, Adams. His lordship has died. You'd better go and tidy yourself up and then come into the house. I want you to make yourself useful and keep an eye on things for me.'

I went back to the cottage and washed and changed. The news, upsetting though it was, was not entirely unexpected. Lord Scarsdale's condition had deteriorated during the past few months. Although I did not mention it in my diary I had, very soon after I started as an estate worker, been asked by Lady Scarsdale if I would look in on his lordship occasionally and keep him company. As an estate worker I was not supposed to be in the house at all. I used to wait until Francis Curzon had gone out in the jeep and the cleaning ladies were out of the way and then I would go to the sitting room where Lord Scarsdale now spent his days. By this time he was in a bad way, unable to speak, unable to dress himself and able to recognise only a few people. He knew me, or rather he knew I was someone he had once known, and he always greeted me with a smile and a chuckle.

Now, after telling Betty the news and tidying myself up, I returned to the Hall. I went first to the sitting room and found Lady Scarsdale and offered her my condolences. She appeared concerned but composed, not weeping. It was perhaps a relief to her.

Lord Scarsdale's end had not been dignified. He had died in the night but his body had not been discovered until the butler went to his bedroom with the breakfast tray at 8.15. He had found him, apparently having suffered a heart attack, lying on the floor in only his pyjama top.

As soon as word went round that Lord Scarsdale had died, everyone was asking how they should now address Mr Curzon. They knew he would be Lord Scarsdale but it did not feel quite right addressing him as such with the old Lord Scarsdale still lying upstairs. I went and asked him what he wished to be called for the time being.

'I know you will be called Lord Scarsdale but does that apply straight away? No one knows the correct procedure.'

He looked at me, raised his hand as if to make an important announcement and said 'The king is dead. Long live the king.'

Oh, I thought, it's to be Your Majesty then. But he went on: 'I am Lord Scarsdale. I am Francis Curzon, 3rd Viscount, 7th Baron

Scarsdale, 13th Baronet. But I don't mind what people call me as long as they're polite.'

The funeral took place the following Monday. I was asked to move the altar from the church, which was far too small to accommodate the large number of mourners, into the Marble Hall and set it up and arrange for as many chairs as possible to be set out. Just before the ceremony began I met Major Chandos Pole, an old family friend.

'Hello, Adams.' We shook hands.

'A sad occasion, sir.'

'Oh, I don't know. He had a bloody good life.'

If not the most tactful expression at that moment, I considered it a better summing up than that which the Bishop of Derby delivered in his eulogy a short while later. Lord Scarsdale had wanted *Moonlight and Roses* played at his funeral. 'Do you know that, Adams?' he had once asked me. 'I've played it many times m'Lord,' I said. But it was not played now; it had associations with his first wife. The family members filed out as the coffin was taken for interment in the little church and Lord Scarsdale was laid to rest among ancestors going back to the 13th century.

After the funeral there was an air of pessimism about the place. No one knew what the new lord's plans were or whether their jobs would be safe. Lady Scarsdale, or rather the now Dowager Lady Scarsdale, had been given six months to make her departure. She had decided to go and live with her son, Mr Bryan, on his estate near Banbury in Oxfordshire. Naturally, she was taking the

Commodore with her and also Mrs Fleetwood and her husband as cook and handyman at the new home.

Most of my time was now spent assisting the new Lord Scarsdale in the house. Although he had been managing the estate for some time, he knew very little about the Hall or its contents. At the same time the Dowager Lady Scarsdale, Tilla, seemed to think she had a right to ask me to do things for her. I had, after all, waited on her for 15 years and in a way we were close. I assisted her in packing up the late Lord Scarsdale's silver and for my help she gave me a plated decanter stand. The Commodore also asked me to help pack some of his things. Tilla wanted me to give her some idea of the value of Lord Scarsdale's collection of arms and armour, which I did. Early the following year the entire collection was sent to Christie's together with a number of Lady Scarsdale's paintings. I moved a collection of sporting prints from the Gun Room and put these in the now empty Armoury Corridor. Already the place was changing.

I was involved with Woofe, the gardener, in making some swaps for Tilla; an iron fire grate of hers and a chest of drawers were exchanged for better ones. We were caught in the act by Lord Scarsdale which made for a very unpleasant time. Lord Scarsdale was obviously worried that Tilla would depart with far more treasures than were legally hers, and not without some cause. From this time on I was witness to and unwillingly caught in their cat and mouse game. Tilla expected me to say nothing of her moves and Lord Scarsdale expected me to act as spy and report all to him.

One day Mrs Payne, Tilla's personal maid, said to me: 'I'm just going along to Aladdin's cave.'

'What on earth do you mean?'

'The old schoolroom. That's where Lady Scarsdale has all the treasures stored that she intends taking with her.'

Just as previously this room had held the Commodore's crates and boxes ready for his retirement, so now it was packed with Tilla's belongings. At times I felt that she was acting quite irrationally and courting trouble and unpleasantness. On one occasion Lord Scarsdale discovered Mrs Payne going along to 'Aladdin's cave' with one of a set of very fine French Empire boudoir chairs from the top landing, and from that time on he became even more suspicious.

'You must be more vigilant, Adams.'

'Well, let me have the inventory, m'Lord, so that I know what belongs to the house and I might make some progress.'

Tilla had given me a copy of her inventory for use when the valuation for probate was done. I took this home to study and found 24 items of silver and plate that I could not account for as her property. It was possible, of course, that she could have acquired certain things during my 10-month absence, but I rather doubted it.

Lord Scarsdale at one time found an inventory of Cross Stitch flat which the Commodore occupied and had furnished himself. Lord Scarsdale was greatly taken up with a wooden coal bucket which he believed belonged to the Hall but which I knew the Commodore had made himself. When I said as much I was accused of disloyalty.

Early in February, Christie's descended on the house. Lord and Lady Scarsdale went off to Scotland but Tilla was like a cat on a hot tin roof most of the time. She flushed the porcelain expert through at great speed. The splendid armorial dinner service which graced the dining room was removed by Partridge's, the auctioneers. But the picture men were more thorough.

Eventually a list of 'Not seen' items was sent by Christie's and Lord Scarsdale asked me to try and locate these. A few seconds' glance at the list showed many 'missing' and 'sold' heirlooms which I knew were still in the house. A 'sold' Marieschi still hung in the dining room and *Man in a dress with gloves* was still in the family wing. I did what I could but it was obvious that a new inventory would have to be drawn up.

In early March, Tilla and the Commodore went off on a holiday to Tobago and I occupied my time with a number of restoration jobs: recaning chairs and repairing the chairs in the estate office.

Christie's came again. This time it was the director of the Oriental Department. I spent an interesting day with him and his team and learnt a lot, particularly about porcelain and rugs.

That April saw the completion of my first year back at Kedleston. In my diary I noted: 'Apart from the days spent with Christie's and the time spent on detective work with the numerous and inadequate lists of heirlooms, the year has been a struggle. I have had to watch Tilla and Lord Scarsdale playing cat and mouse; I have had to listen to the moans and groans and suspicions of the staff; and I have been sickened by the whole atmosphere of the place. But I take consolation from the fact that Betty is helped financially and that my hurt pride has mended a little.'

Tilla finally departed at the end of July, calmly and without fuss. I think she must have felt relief and sadness together. For myself, in the now quiet house I felt a strange emptiness. I thought of past days and years and realised all I had given amounted to nothing. All I had was foreboding for the future.

CHAPTER 24

The family wing was now silent and stripped of most of its furniture. Tilla and the Commodore had gone and the cook and her husband with them. The lady's maid was no longer needed. Out of season the state rooms were locked and the Indian Museum closed. Lord Scarsdale continued to live at Weston Lodge. He had told me once that he would never live in Kedleston Hall when he succeeded to the title and inherited the property.

I was left largely to my own devices. Lord Scarsdale's instructions were merely: 'Keep an eye on things'. Now and again he would grumble that he could not find enough for me to do. He rarely came into the house, working still from his office in the stable yard. I was now based in the Gun Room on the ground floor of the central part of the house, adjacent to Caesars' Hall. It was a dark, ill-equipped room and there were no tools to work with.

After about a year it became apparent that Lord Scarsdale had decided he would now live at the Hall. He began an extensive programme of alterations and improvements in the family wing. The old boilers which I had attended to as houseman were ripped out and replaced with an oil-fired central heating system. Half the old kitchen floor was removed and replaced, and a new cooker and kitchen units were fitted. Bathrooms were modernised and the whole wing redecorated throughout.

I was in the Gun Room one morning when Lord Scarsdale came in, quite obviously in one of his better moods. After a few minutes' chat he said that when they moved in they would need a man to look after them and did I know of anyone. 'Someone we can rely on and trust to look after us,' he added. I could see where this was leading. On an earlier occasion Lady Helene Scarsdale had said to me that they always assumed I would carry on after Lord Richard died and work for them as butler.

I now told Lord Scarsdale that I did not know of anyone and that I could not offer my own services as I felt I had already given all I could to the family and the house, and was too near retirement to start again. He accepted this but expressed his disappointment.

I could have become their butler; my health was better then. But I thought: they have two young sons to look after and they are starting a new life. It will be too much for me.

Even before Lord Scarsdale moved in, the Hall was not entirely empty. There were a number of parts of the house itself which had been converted with varying degrees of success and let out as flats. There were long-term tenants in what was known as China Flat, on the ground floor of the central part of the house, adjacent to the Indian Museum. And there were three flats on the first and second floors of the West Wing, occupied by a young married couple, an elderly lady and a woman who worked at Derby Museum. But in the vastness of the place it was easy to imagine I was entirely alone in the deserted Hall with only ghosts of the past for company. There was plenty of time for reflection.

At such times I would go back over the years with their hundreds of memories and think of all those things I had done beyond the call of duty. I had nursed the sick, comforted the dying, changed babies' nappies, placated cooks, dealt with amorous intrigues, exercised gun dogs, assisted the elderly at bath-time, cooked meals, coped with fire and flood, buried family pets, painted almost every inch of the place, acted as chauffeur, restored furniture, carried arms to Birmingham with an Irish woman beside me at the height of the terrorist campaign, and had been expected to know the answer to everything – even to crossword clues.

Like many old houses, Kedleston has its collection of legends. One of these is a story that centuries earlier gypsies had come begging for water for their horses and had been refused. The gypsies laid a curse upon the people of the house. Sometimes I could not help thinking that, whoever it was intended for, the curse had fallen not on the Curzons but on the people who worked for them.

But at the time I could still write in my diary: 'I hope this will be the end of a miserable period for both Betty and myself and the beginning of happier times.'

EPILOGUE

But better times did not follow. Roy's wife died in 1980 after a short illness. He remarried in 1982 and continued to work at the Hall until he became seriously ill in 1987. By this time the National Trust had taken over the property. Roy recovered but never completely regained his health. He worked for a time as a furniture restorer and continued to live at Brook Willows in Kedleston village. In response to many requests and urgings from family and friends he eventually began to recount his memories, and his wife shaped them into the pages you have read. Roy died in Cheltenham in 2008, aged 86.